'Tom Mole's enthusiasm for books is infectious. If you also love books . . . you'll want to discover *The Secret Life of Books*.'
– Sam Jordison, author of *Literary London*

'A treat for bibliophiles everywhere.'
– Gavin Francis, author of *Shapeshifters*

'A treasure-chest, filled with bookish wonders.'
– Adam Roberts, author of *Jack Glass*

'I suspect I'll never look at a book the same way again'
– Jon Courtenay Grimwood, author of *Stamping Butterflies*

D1363061

THE
secret
LIFE
OF books

Why they mean more than words

TOM MOLE

Elliott&Thompson

First published 2019 by
Elliott and Thompson Limited
2 John Street
London WC1N 2ES
www.eandtbooks.com

This paperback edition first published in 2020

ISBN: 978-1-78396-529-8

9 8 7 6 5 4 3 2 1

A catalogue record for this book is available from the British Library.

Typesetting: Marie Doherty
Printed by CPI Group (UK) Ltd, Croydon, CR0 4YY

'O tempora! O lectores!'[1]

CHARLES LAMB

To Freya

CONTENTS

ILLUSTRATIONS

BOOK/BOOK

*The things we do to books and
the things they do to us*

When I was a student, one of my professors was almost driven out of his office by his books. He had a large room on the ground floor of the English department, with bookcases around the walls. Slowly but surely these bookcases had filled over the years, and other shelves had been squeezed into every available space in the office. The bookcases had started to sprout out from the walls into the room, creating book booths, book niches and book nooks. But these, in turn, proved insufficient for his ever-growing collection of books. Soon he started to pile books on top of the bookcases, and to stack them double on the shelves, so that he had to move the books in front in order to reveal the ones behind. Before long, the books had spilled onto the floor, where the piles encroached further and further into the room with each passing month.

Every time I visited the professor's office, it seemed a little harder than before to navigate a route across the room on the decreasing area of visible carpet. Attempting to keep the books in some kind of order seemed like a full-time job. I'd knock on the professor's door and hear a muffled shout telling me to come in. But when I opened the door there was no professor to be seen – the room was full of books, but apparently empty of its occupant. For a moment, I would think perhaps the professor had been crushed under a toppling pile of hardbacks. Then his head would appear from behind a ziggurat of volumes on a bewildering variety of topics. 'Just doing a bit of sorting out,' he'd say, as though he could ever hope to bring order to the ever-growing library that seemed, like the universe itself, to be continually expanding at an accelerating rate in every possible direction.

My professor was doing a number of things to his books. He was acquiring them – choosing to buy these books rather than others. He was classifying them – putting them onto shelves and into piles with other books. These categories might be based on some quality such as their subject matter (history on one shelf, biography on another), or their size (larger books on the floor, smaller ones on the shelves), or their place in the cycle of his reading (as-yet-unread ones over here; the ones he was currently reading over there; the ones he had finished reading but not yet shelved somewhere else). He was reading them, taking notes from them, referring back to them, citing them in the articles he was writing, using them to prepare his lectures, lending them to his students, and so on in an endless process of erudition and amusement.

But his books were also doing things to him. As well as pushing him out of his own office, they were shaping the spaces and the ways in which he worked. The books formed a complex ecosystem that he, too, inhabited. Sometimes, they made his work easier and better. Writing scholarly articles amid such a large private library allowed him to keep reference works, books by other scholars and the literature he was writing about within easy reach. All scholarship depends to some extent on other scholarship – even when it reaches different conclusions – and so the thousands of books he kept to hand assisted his work. Sometimes, on the other hand, the sheer number of books and their disorganised state must have made things more difficult. It must often have been tricky or impossible to find the book he wanted.

Eventually the department secretary decided enough was enough and sent in a structural engineer to test whether the building could take the weight of so many books. Armed with the engineer's report, she persuaded the professor to give some books away. (He gave one to me.) But it was hard to convince him to downsize his library. His professional life, indeed his understanding of himself, was ranged around the shelves for all to see. Giving up some of his books felt like giving up part of his mind. There were benefits and difficulties in having such a large collection of books. But, for better or worse, his books were not just his passive tools; they were also exerting forces of their own on his life.

⁓

Sometimes, we think of books as tools for reading, but there's more to them than that. In this book – the one you're reading now – I'm not all that interested in books as things to read. Instead, I want to talk about all the other things that we do to books – and that books do to us. Our books are leading a double life. As well as being containers of words, they are things imbued with their own significance. Their importance – as my professor understood – goes far beyond the words or images they contain.

Books are part of how we understand ourselves. They shape our identities, even before we can read them. They accompany us throughout our lives – at home, at school, at college and (for some of us, at least) at work. And books are also part of how we relate to other people, from those closest to us to those only distantly connected. They get tangled up in our relationships with parents, siblings, classmates, teachers, friends, lovers and children. They are part of how groups of people, and even whole nations, imagine and represent themselves. Books become meaningful objects in all sorts of ways: treasured possessions, talismans, bearers of significance. This book is about how that happens.

For readers, books are familiar objects. Maybe we're too familiar with them to pay them much attention. We take them to bed with us. They weigh down our suitcases when we go on holiday. We display them on our bookshelves or store them in our attics. We give them as gifts. We write our names in them. We hoard them or discard them. We take them for granted. Over the last five hundred years, printed books have become a common sight – so common that they are almost invisible. It requires an effort, a shift of perspective, to bring them into focus.

Today, we can make that effort because it has become possible to imagine the end of the book as we know it. We can perceive the book as an object because we think that object might be going away. When historians of the future look back to the early twenty-first century, they will describe it as a moment of media change as significant as the Western invention of printing with movable type in the second half of the fifteenth century. But as the epoch of print ends, printed books are not simply vanishing; instead, their significance is being transformed. We're historically well placed to understand this transformation.

And yet we often fail to understand it. If we think of books as just media – just a way of conveying text and images – then we'll expect them to give way to new media that do the job faster, more cheaply, more efficiently or more profitably. The strange tenacity of the paper book will seem puzzling. But once we understand the life of books as objects, and the many functions they serve in our lives, then we'll be better equipped to understand what's happening to them now.

～

Think about one of your favourite books. What springs to mind? You probably remember nuggets of content: episodes in the story, favourite characters or choice quotations. You might also recollect where and when you read the book – on a pleasant holiday, a long plane ride, a commuter train, a lazy Sunday. You might associate the book with a particular time of your life and recall how it made you feel or what it made you think. Or you might remember where you bought it, or who recommended it or gave it to you.

Perhaps you also recall something about the book as a physical object. Your memories might include some recollection of the picture on the cover, some scarcely formed awareness of what the typeface was like to read, or some muscle memory of how the book felt in your hands. These physical features often seem less important, because we've learned to think of them as incidental to the business of books and reading. What's important, we think, is what the book says, not what it looks like, what it smells like or what it feels like to hold.

We've been taught to think this way from an early age. Learning to read means learning to stop looking at the book in front of us and to start looking through it. As we come to think of books as simply strings of signs to decipher so that we can get at the stories, the ideas or the information they convey, we learn to ignore their physical features. We're told not to judge a book by its cover. We think that only children's books have pictures (which until quite recently was certainly not the case), and we're keen to move on to reading grown-up books, with only words. As a result, we start to treat the book simply as a container of information, a device for delivering narratives. The book itself starts to vanish, to seem as though it's hardly a thing at all. As we gain the ability to lose ourselves in a book, the book as an object begins to get lost.

〜〜

This relationship between the ignorable material form of a book and its valuable content might remind us of another familiar relationship: that between body and soul. The words in the book are to its material form as the immortal soul is to the mortal body. Words can leave behind their material existence in the book, and migrate to new forms, just as souls can leave behind their worldly incarnations and take on new, heavenly bodies. And while the book (like the body) is subject to various infirmities and imperfections – misprints, cracked spines, torn pages, dog-eared corners – the work (like the soul) transcends it. The American founding father Benjamin Franklin played with this idea when he composed his own jokey epitaph. Franklin, who was a printer in Philadelphia, likened his dead body to 'the Cover of an old Book, / Its Contents torn out, / And stript of its Lettering and Gilding'. And he likened his soul to the book's contents. 'But the Work shall not be wholly lost,' he wrote, 'For it will, as he believ'd, appear once more, / In a new & more perfect Edition, / Corrected and Amended / By the Author.'

In order to resist this tendency to look down on the book as an object and look up at its content, we need to make a conscious effort to focus on the 'thingness' of the book. You can start making that effort now, using this book as a starting point. As you turn over this page, feel the paper between your fingers, notice the look of the type, the smell the book gives off, the heft of the volume in your hand. Or, if you're reading on a digital device, notice how that experience differs from reading a paper book. Look at the options for changing the font or the size of the text, feel the size and shape of the device. Take a moment to do it now.

Making that effort allows us to see how our books shape the ways in which we read them. As objects, books are constantly sending us messages about how we should approach the texts they contain. Weighty hardbacks printed on thick paper with sober covers tell us to take them seriously. They are designed to last, allowing their text to be read many times. Detective stories printed on cheap paper with flimsy bindings and garish covers shout at us to buy them, read them fast and throw them away. If you try to reread them more than a couple of times they will literally fall to pieces. Poetry volumes surround a well-turned sonnet with acres of white margin, like a piece of polished jet displayed on an ample white cushion. The page layout entreats us to bring to the poem a mind cleared of distractions, like the page, and focused tightly on the words islanded in a sea of white space. When you read a book, you're always reading a material object as well as a string of text. Reading matter always takes the form of, well, matter.

Paying this kind of attention to the book as an object also reveals the purposes books serve in society. We use books for a lot of things besides reading. They serve as badges of allegiance, identifying the bearer as part of a group of readers who are devoted to a particular kind of book. They can be insignia of class, indicating the social position of their owners in complex ways. They can become the focus of rituals and celebrations. Literary festivals take place across the world, bringing together authors, readers and booksellers around the object of the book. Some books even have celebrations specifically focused on them, like the midnight launch events for Harry Potter books that attracted queues of costumed readers eager for the next instalment. Books can function as tokens shaping interpersonal relationships, for example when they are given as gifts or prizes. They can be a link between parents and children, for example when reading aloud at bedtime. They can bring people together in book clubs and reading groups. Considered in this light, the book starts to appear as a lively object, with its own vibrant social life.

Books are a great example of how objects of all kinds take on meanings.[1] Coats, cars, hamburgers, shoes – these things all carry meanings that extend well beyond their purpose as clothing, transport, food or footwear. The safe, dependable Volvo, the flashy Mercedes and the second-hand Toyota all tell us things about their owners that have nothing to do with their desire to get from A to B. These meanings vary from one time and place to another. In one society a second-hand Toyota might be rather *déclassé*; in a less-privileged one it might be the zenith of luxury. And the meanings of things take shape in relation to the meanings of other things. A Mercedes would not be a sign of status if it were the only kind of car you could buy.[2]

Books are no different – in fact they are a particularly good example of how things become bearers of meanings. Imagine three copies of *Jane Eyre*. One is a cheap paperback, bought from a cardboard box on the pavement outside a second-hand bookstore (this is the rusty Toyota of the book-shelf). The other is a hefty new hardback, bought from a large

well-lit bookshop (this is the Volvo, solid and reliable). The
third is a leather-bound copy of the first edition signed by
its author, and bought from a major auction house (this is a
very smart Mercedes, or maybe a Ferrari). All three contain
Charlotte Brontë's novel. But all three offer drastically different reading experiences (if, that is, they are read at all). They
represent different kinds of investment on the part of their
owners – in terms of money, time and emotional energy –
and so they are treated in different ways, and come to mean
different things.

Shelves of antiquarian volumes in leather bindings signify
one thing, a stack of second-hand paperbacks on a bedside
table another. And the same volume can take on different con-
notations when used in different settings, at different times
and in different ways. A textbook from the eighteenth century
– carried to class by a student who scribbled notes to his class-
mate in the margins when the teacher bored him, or tried out
his pen on the endpapers to see if the nib wrote well – might
become the centrepiece of a twenty-first-century collector's
library. A paperback novel thrown aside by a businessman
after a long-haul flight might make its way to a charity shop

and become the treasured possession of a child with a thirst for reading but little money for books.

We haven't grasped the meanings of books if we think of them only as things to read. The Oxford philosopher Gilbert Ryle coined the term 'thick description'.[3] Think about how we might describe a coat. The coat keeps its wearer warm. That's an accurate description, but it's a 'thin' one. To offer a 'thick' description, we need to pay attention to a much fuller range of meanings. The coat might signal things about its wearer's job (a doctor's white coat), her wealth and social status (a cashmere overcoat), his membership of a group (a biker's leather jacket) and so on. So, to say that books are containers of words or tools for reading is an accurate description, but Ryle would say it's a 'thin' one. A thick description of the book would include a much wider set of meanings.

But books don't just *mean* things to us. They also *do* things to us. The doctor's training and expertise give her the authority to wear the white coat, but the coat doesn't just reflect authority; it also confers it. The doctor without the white coat looks like anyone else. With it, she commands a certain respect; people treat her differently. When she's wearing the coat, perhaps she carries herself differently or speaks more confidently too. So, the white coat is doing something, both to the doctor and to those around her.

Books, too, are doing things to those who encounter them.

~~~

In its long history, the book has taken a variety of forms and employed a wide array of materials. There are books in cuneiform writing from the ancient Sumerian empire, made by pushing a stylus into clay tablets. Others were written on papyrus made from reeds growing along the Nile in ancient Egypt, or inscribed on bamboo strips in China. Books were printed from carved wooden blocks in China by 868 CE and possibly much earlier, as well as in Korea and Japan. In medieval Europe, books were written on parchment made from animal skins and decorated with coloured inks and gold leaf. Printing with metal type developed, apparently independently, in both Asia and Europe. As early as the thirteenth century, artisans at the Korean court were experimenting with copper moveable type. By the end of the fifteenth century, books were being printed in Europe using lead type to transfer ink onto paper made from linen rags.

Printing spread across Europe from Germany to Italy, France, Spain, Poland, England, Belgium, Sweden and Turkey (all before 1500). It was exported to South America in the early 1500s and North America by the beginning of the following century. Printing in the Middle East dates from the early 1600s in Lebanon, although the Quran was printed in Arabic type in Venice as early as 1514. Colonists and missionaries carried printing presses and moveable type to India, Africa, Australia and New Zealand in the eighteenth century. Printing developed along slightly different lines in East Asia. Because the printers were working with written languages consisting of thousands of characters, rather than the limited Western alphabet, they tended to prefer wooden type (xylography), which was cheaper to produce and easier to alter. Using these methods, Chinese, Japanese and Korean printers sustained a great expansion in publishing long before Europe experienced a similar phenomenon.

Over time, printing slowly became industrialised, until in nineteenth-century Europe steam-driven presses were producing hundreds of pages an hour, on paper made by machines from esparto grass and wood pulp. These developments made books cheaper and more widely available, and increasing literacy levels allowed books to reach across the social spectrum. The invention of the paperback in the twentieth century made the book more affordable, more portable and – often – more disposable. Books have come in many shapes and sizes, been produced for many purposes, and employed many different kinds of material.[4]

In what follows, I'll look back to that history to see what it can tell us about how books function as objects. But this book is written with both eyes on the present. For that reason, it's largely about the kind of book that's most familiar to us today: the printed codex. The codex form emerged long before print, in the first centuries of the Common Era. It consists of a series of leaves stacked on top of one another and gathered together along one edge. In other words, it's the book as we know it now. The book in your hands – if you're reading the paper version rather than the e-book – is a codex, just like (I'm fairly sure) more or less all the paper books you will have encountered.

Early readers of the codex praised it for being portable and easy to handle compared with the scroll. It allows a reader to flick through the pages and dip in and out, in a way that isn't so easy to do with a scroll that has to be unrolled and rolled up again. Despite these advantages, however, the codex took a long time to catch on. The evidence of surviving books suggests that it slowly gained ground over the scroll between about 100 and 500 CE. It's not a coincidence that these were the years when Christianity was also gaining converts. Christians were early adopters of the codex. They helped to refine the techniques required to make codices (the plural of codex), and they particularly favoured the codex form for their scriptures. As Christianity became more widespread, so the Christians' preferred form of the book also took off.

Printing is the other key element of the book as we know it. In Europe, its story begins with the prodigiously bearded goldsmith and entrepreneur Johannes Gutenberg, who invented movable type and the printing press around 1439. (Movable type had been invented independently in Asia long before this date, but Gutenberg almost certainly didn't know this.) Gutenberg developed his printing press from earlier presses used for producing olive oil or wine. He used the skills he had developed as a goldsmith to create little pieces of lead with individual letters formed in relief on the top. The letters were reversed, so that they appeared the right way round when printed. Gutenberg arranged his pieces of type to spell out words, and then applied ink to the raised parts of the letters. (This was done with a dabber, and a skilled printer who could apply the ink evenly became known as a 'dab hand'.) A sheet of paper was laid on top of the inked type. The press applied pressure, pushing the paper down and causing ink to transfer onto the paper. The combination of movable type and the printing press was the breakthrough that allowed numerous copies of a text to be produced much faster than copying by hand. Printing wasn't used just for books. From the beginning a range of other things were printed, including forms, receipts, broadsides and posters.

The book as we know it today is the product of a marriage between the form of the codex and the technology of print. People are still producing manuscript books (think of diaries, notebooks or handwritten collections of recipes), and there are still some books that aren't codices (think of concertina books for children, or the Torah scroll used in synagogues). But for several hundred years the printed codex has been the default form for circulating and storing text.

For a long time, books and their users – whether those users are readers or writers, buyers or sellers, borrowers or lenders – have shared a bookish ecosystem that has proved to be extraordinarily robust, enduring times of turbulence such as wars, famines and plagues. Sometimes, in fact, the book thrives in these conditions – the annual output of printed books and pamphlets in English actually went up during the English Civil War, as controversial pamphlets on current affairs streamed from the press, waging war in print as well as on the battlefield. As I'll suggest later, this ecosystem has accommodated new media (such as photography) with ease and learned to operate alongside other media such as radio, cinema and television.

But now the printed codex is being displaced from the position of cultural centrality that it has held in the West for the last five hundred years. Digital technologies are challenging the role of print as our default medium for text. Meanwhile, new media are changing the habits of attention that the printed book fostered. Today, many of us read more on the screen than we do on the page, using a variety of devices: some designed for reading books (e-readers) and some designed primarily for other purposes (phones, tablets, laptops). It's a brave new world that has such books in it. Reports of the death of the book are probably not just premature but also simplistic and overstated. But that doesn't mean we should underestimate the challenge of the digital. If digital technologies are changing the book beyond recognition, now is the time to consider what we might lose as we embrace them.

It may be a mistake to generalise about the paper book, drawing up battle lines with all the paper books on one side and all the e-books on the other. Books are too various, too different from one another, and they serve too many different purposes to be corralled into convenient oppositions in this way. Looking along my shelves, I can see reference books for looking up facts, detective novels for entertainment, academic monographs I use in my work as a researcher, textbooks and anthologies I use as a teacher (or that I used as a student), art books more for looking at than for reading, children's books I read aloud to my daughter, slim volumes of poetry, a Bible in a slip case, and many more. The printed codex has been so successful in part because it's flexible enough to be used for a variety of different kinds of book.

People acquire 'bookish' tastes in response to particular con-stellations of circumstances. There weren't many books in my house when I was growing up. We had a Bible and a complete works of Shakespeare, items as familiar in English houses as a teapot and tea strainer (but not used so often). There was a textbook belonging to my dad called *Advanced Air Conditioning and Refrigeration*, which was kept in a cupboard because it didn't seem the kind of book anyone wanted to display on a shelf. There were one or two cookbooks. There was a mawkish volume of poetry called *Poems of Love and Reflection*; no one seemed to know how this had got into the house. That was about it. My parents owned few books of their own. But they associated books with education, and education with advancement of all kinds – social, professional and financial. All of which, apparently, we could do with. I also had the good fortune to live in an area that was well provided with public libraries and to attend a state school with a well-appointed library. My interest in books stems at least in part from this particular context, and the aspirations it fostered.

As a schoolboy studying English, it didn't occur to me to want to own the books I was reading in class. Sometimes we had to buy books, but for the most part the teacher gave books out at the beginning of term and collected them in at the end. And nor did it seem remarkable that the school would buy so many copies of the same book. Sometimes these books were new, when the budget allowed or the curriculum changed, but often they bore the marks of previous pupils' engagement with the text – or their disengagement from it, as they doodled in the margins while bored in class. We worked through these books carefully and slowly, and I can still remember many details from them. I probably still know *Macbeth*, which I studied as a sixteen-year-old, better than any other Shakespeare play. I can remember the edition we used, which had a photograph from a recent production of the play on the cover. But I gave that book back at the end of term without a second thought.

It wasn't until I became a postgraduate student that I needed more than one small bookcase to hold my books. By then, books were becoming an important part of how I spent my time and money. Slowly, my aspirations took shape – I hoped to get a PhD, and perhaps to become an academic. One day, I hoped to write a book of my own. Books were now my business. I spent my working days surrounded by them in the library. But I also bought books and kept them at home. This was in the early days of shopping for second-hand books on the internet, and I was able to buy cheaply some of the academic monographs I was reading for my doctorate. Even if my ambitions to become an academic came to nothing, I figured I'd at least have a shelf of books to remind me of the time I'd spent immersed in my thesis. One afternoon, passing by an office building that was being renovated, I spotted two cheap white bookcases that looked as if they were being thrown out. They were chipped and a little wonky. The workmen decorating the offices said I could have them for free, and a friend with a van helped me get them back to my flat. As the bookcases filled, so my doctoral thesis took shape. Eventually, a bound copy of my thesis and later still the book that I wrote based on it took their places on the shelves.

Since then, I've continued to buy and read books, as well as to write them. And my work has taken me to libraries where

I've been lucky enough to handle some real treasures. Buying books, reading them, organising them and referring back to them – all these things seem to me distinct and different kinds of pleasure. I'm not a collector so much as an accumulator of books. I have a few modest antiquarian volumes, but most of my books are paperbacks I bought new and then hung on to. I doubt I would have kept so many books if they hadn't served some ulterior purposes that aren't apparent even to me. I was the first in my immediate family to go to university, and I suspect the books on my shelves reassure me that I really have learned something along the way. Like the certificates on the wall in a doctor's surgery or a lawyer's office, they offer a kind of proof that I'm more or less qualified to teach and write about literature and book history. Perhaps by writing this book about books I'm hoping to convince myself once and for all.

2

BOOK/THING

How books function as objects
circulating among other objects

Sometimes, the moment when you can see the book most clearly as an object is the moment when it stops working as it's supposed to. When I was an undergraduate, trying to finish George Eliot's novel *Middlemarch* for class the following day, I turned a page partway through the book to discover that I'd gone back in time. I was rereading sentences that I distinctly remembered reading earlier that morning. No longer absorbed in the story, I looked more closely at another aspect of the book – its page numbers – and discovered that instead of page 140 being followed by page 141, it was actually followed by a second copy of page 109. (I hadn't got all that far in.) As I flipped through a few more pages, it became clear that a whole chunk of the text had been duplicated, and that a corresponding chunk was missing. The time of the story was out of joint, its characters stranded in limbo, compelled to repeat their actions of thirty pages earlier. I wasn't going to be able to read the novel in time for class unless I found another copy. These days, I could simply have gone online to find the text but back then I had to go out to a library or bookshop to find a replacement.

As a vehicle for delivering the text of *Middlemarch*, my book had broken down. But in that moment it was also revealed to me in a new light. I was no longer able to ignore the physical form of the book, to treat it as just a window to the words. Instead, the book reappeared as a thing. I thought – really for the first time – about how it had been made in a factory by machines. I noticed that it was the product of technologies and processes about which I knew very little. I became aware that fallible individuals had manufactured it. I realised that the book had been assembled from several different parts, and that in this case some of those parts had got mixed up. Quite suddenly, I perceived the book in my hands as an object, in a way that hadn't previously occurred to me.

And it was also clear, in that moment, that this copy of *Middlemarch* was unlike others that purported to be the same. Different editions of the same novel, and even other copies of the same edition, didn't have the same problem as this copy. Although they all seemed to offer the same experience – the experience of reading Eliot's novel – that experience differed according to the particular book the reader encountered the novel in. As a communications technology, my book had crashed. But other books contained bugs and glitches that we put up with quite happily: misprints or misnumbered pages, and, as their lives went on, pages stained, dog-eared, ripped or torn out altogether. Although I'd read plenty of books, these were things I'd scarcely given any thought to before. Only when my book broke down did it become impossible to take it for granted.

Quite a long time after that, I discovered that this experience, in which an object becomes visible as such when it stops working as it's intended to, was one that I apparently shared with the philosopher Martin Heidegger.[1] His example is a hammer. When you're using a hammer and everything is going well, you don't think about the hammer, only the business of hammering. Stop to think about the hammer, and the chances are you'll hit your own thumb. It's only when the hammer breaks, Heidegger suggests, that the carpenter's relationship to it changes. In that moment, the hammer loses its 'equipmentality' (the unlovely term coined to translate Heidegger's word *Zeugsein*), and it becomes visible to the carpenter as a thing.

The same is true of books. They tend to disappear when in use. In that moment when we're fully absorbed in a book, we experience a kind of direct access to the author's words, the author's imagined world, even the author's thoughts, that can seem almost mystical in nature. The medium does its job most effectively when it becomes most transparent. We stop noticing the book and become immersed in the work it contains. This is a sort of ecstasy, in the distinctive historical sense of going outside of oneself, into a kind of swoon, or trance, or heightened state of consciousness. As we enter the author's world, we lose sight of the book as an object.

Marcel Proust, in his essay 'On Reading', provides a wonderful description of this kind of submersion in a book. Proust recounts how, as a child, he retreated in the morning to the dining room, where he planned to read in a chair by the fire until lunchtime. But the cook came in to lay the table for lunch and disturbed him:

[S]he thought she had to say, 'You're not comfortable like that; what if I brought you a table?' And just to answer: 'No, thank you' you had to stop short and bring back from afar your voice which from within your lips was repeating noiselessly, hurriedly, all the words your eyes had read; you had to stop it, make it be heard, and, in order to say properly, 'No, thank you', give it an appearance of ordinary life, the intonation of an answer, which it had lost.[2]

Proust celebrates the book's ability to transport its reader to another place, as the reader's body is colonised by the author and his voice is no longer his own. The passage is a favourite among readers who celebrate the slightly uncanny pleasure of being absorbed in a story. Perhaps the experience is especially intense for children; I know I sometimes have to say my daughter's name several times in order to bring her out of storyland and back to the real world. But Proust has little to say about the book he's reading – is it large or small, heavy or light, new or old, thick or thin, colourful or plain, tattered or pristine? His prose – usually so profligate with details – has nothing to say about these matters.

The cook – whose labours leave her no time for reading that morning – sees things differently. While the young

Marcel is lost in the book's contents, the cook responds to it as an object. It must be heavy. Perhaps it's too large for the small boy to handle comfortably. Wouldn't a table make things easier? Her concerns are resolutely practical. It is precisely because she's excluded from reading the book by her class, her gender and her job that the cook sees it as an object. In this sense, she's better attuned to my topic than the young Proust, for whom the book has entirely disappeared in the experience of its reading. I enjoy that experience of immersion as much as any reader. But I also think we might try to take a step back from it to allow the book to become the object of our attention in a different way, as it is for the Proust family's cook, and as it became for me that day reading *Middlemarch*. When books stop serving us as tools or interfaces, they also start to come into view as things.

My experience with *Middlemarch* that day stayed with me for a long time, and changed the way I looked at books for ever. Once I started really to pay attention to books, rather than just looking at the words they contained, I realised how much my books had been marked by how I used them. The wrinkles along the spine of my copy of *Middlemarch* showed how far

I'd read before the book broke down. A poetry anthology fell open at a favourite poem. Cookbooks showed fingerprints on favourite recipes. Cake recipes had acquired cocoa-coloured smudges, while curry recipes were redolent of spices stuck between the pages. Like clothes or shoes that start off as identical copies and mould to their owners' bodies over time, books get worn in. Once I started to pay attention to books as objects, I began to see traces of how those objects had been used. Or not used – some books that I really should have read still look suspiciously pristine on the shelf.

Books don't reveal how they've been used only by their current owners; they sometimes carry scars from past encounters as well. In *Far from the Madding Crowd* (1874), Thomas Hardy describes a family Bible whose pages have been quite worn away in popular passages by 'unpractised readers in former days' dragging their fingers along under the words as they read.[3] Taking up the Bible reveals the semi-literate state of its earlier readers, as well as the passages that most interested them. To the careful observer, the book can be excavated like an archaeological dig, revealing layer upon layer of information about its previous users from the material traces they left behind them.

Different people handle their books in different ways, and so leave different kinds of traces. The more I looked at books, the more I learned to recognise these traces. The editor and essayist Anne Fadiman distinguishes between two kinds of book-lover: the 'courtly' and the 'carnal'.[4] When I read her description, I remembered two university friends who exemplified the two types. They even looked like opposites: the courtly book-lover was tall, slender and blonde; the carnal book-lover was short, full-figured and dark-haired.

The courtly book-lover bought nice editions and did her best to preserve them in pristine condition. She had a little ritual that I've never known anyone else perform. When she got a new paperback, she stood it on its spine on the table in front of her, and then, taking a small gathering of the first and last pages between each thumb and forefinger, she eased them down towards the table. Then she took two gatherings nearer the centre of the book and did the same, and so on, fanning the pages out gently as she worked her way towards the mid-point of the volume. In this way, she softened and flexed the spine before she started reading the book. The spine stayed smooth and firm as a result, instead of cracking or creasing where it had been recklessly bent backwards somewhere midway through the book at a particularly exciting moment in the plot. Her books stood resplendent on her shelves, looking almost as clean and bright as they had in the shop. Needless to say, she never wrote in them.

The carnal book-lover, on the other hand, could never have brought herself to perform the spine-softening ritual. It would have meant deferring the pleasure of reading the book. She pounced on a new book and devoured it. Dog-eared corners held no fear for her. Cracked spines, biro marks in the margins and on the endpapers, coffee stains on the cover – these were all simply marks of affection, signs of the intensity of her love for the book. If she left a book open face down on her bedside table, it just meant that she could pick it up more easily and start reading where she had left off. Her favourite books were her tattiest, because she had read them to death. She had no interest in preserving her books in pristine condition: she wanted them to look as if they'd been read.

When these two book-lovers saw each other's bookshelves, they recoiled in dismay. 'How can you possibly treat your books like that?' asked the courtly lover, surveying the cracked and creased spines of her carnal counterpart's books. 'Don't you have any respect for them?' The carnal lover, facing the bookcase of her courtly opposite number, said, 'Have you actually read any of these books? It certainly doesn't look like it.' And so they would part company, each shaking her head at the other's misguided approach to books.

The more I looked at books for traces of how they'd been read, the more evidence I found of their past adventures with other owners and readers. I started to love old books for their accumulated signs of use as much as I loved new books for their pristine sense of potential. I also realised that reading isn't the only thing we do with books, or the only thing that leaves traces on them.[5] The travel writer and Second World War hero Patrick Leigh Fermor, for example, liked to paste envelopes into the back covers of his books, which he would fill with letters from friends, notes, newspaper clippings and other relevant scraps. He described his habit in a 1982 letter like this:

My system is to cut the flap off an envelope, then stick it with UHU [glue] inside the backboard of the book, with the now un-flapped opening facing *upwards*, but *inwards*, so that the contents can't fall out. It makes the book much more interesting later on, is great fun to do and fills one with a feeling of achievement; and it is hard to imagine a more insidious and time-wasting excuse for postponing what you really ought to be doing. Start today.[6]

In this way, Leigh Fermor added interest and value to his books. Returning to the same volumes and adding more snippets to their envelopes over a number of years, he developed long-term relationships with his books that made them into a swelling archive of scraps and slips. Reading his books was only the beginning.

He wasn't the only one to turn his books into a kind of filing system, or to use them as a set of safety deposit boxes. Giuseppe Tomasi di Lampedusa, the aristocratic Sicilian author of *The Leopard* (1958), wrote a letter to his adopted son in which he identified the real-life people on whom he'd based the characters in the novel. This was in the spring of 1957, when the novel was still unpublished, and he was about to leave for Rome to be treated for the tumour on his lung that would kill him a few weeks later. His wife had picked up Lampedusa's own habit of putting important documents into books in their extensive library for safekeeping. She put his letter into a volume of *The Voyages of Captain Cook* and forgot all about it. It remained undisturbed between the pages of the book for forty-seven years, until it was rediscovered in 2000.[7]

In both these examples, books serve purposes besides reading, even for keen readers. In other cases, reading the book may simply be beside the point. The important thing about a book might be its rarity, or the beauty of its binding, or the quality of its craftsmanship, or the identity of a former owner. The text it contains is almost irrelevant. Some people give, display, examine or appreciate books without ever reading them. I once met a rich New Yorker who collected books with fore-edge paintings – decorations along the front edges of the pages, visible only when the book is closed. She didn't even open her expensive books, let alone read them. She was quite happy to spend huge sums of money on books written in languages she couldn't understand, or on subjects she had no interest in. For her, the text on the pages was neither here nor there; the object of the book was everything.

~~~

I soon realised that, if I wanted to understand the secret life of books as things, I needed to pay attention to how books appeared in public as well as how they were used in private. Books aren't just personal possessions; they are also focal points for a number of social rituals. Holy books are the most obvious example. In public worship, the veneration due to the scripture often overflows onto the object that contains it. Jewish tradition prescribes that the Torah used in synagogues should be a scroll, not a codex. The scroll is handled with great respect, and kept in the Ark of the synagogue. In many Christian churches, the Bible is ritually brought in and out of the church, and ceremonially read from during the service. Some Muslims believe that they should undertake a ritual cleansing before touching a copy of the Quran. The respect that believers give to the scripture is not limited to the words but extends to the books as objects, which get invested with a certain dignity of their own.

This dignity extends beyond houses of worship into other contexts. In many countries, law courts ask witnesses to swear on the Bible or some other holy book (despite occasional misgivings by Christians who recall Jesus's words in the Gospel of Matthew (5:34), 'Do not take an oath at all'). The courts invest the object of the book with a quasi-magical power to make people tell the truth: when a barrister reminds a witness that they are 'under oath', she is not just warning them that they may be guilty of perjury if they lie, but also invoking the power of a certain form of words, spoken over a book, to make them tell the truth in the first place. Notice, again, how little this has to do with actually reading the book. Every day, people who have read little or none of the Bible swear oaths on it in court.

In some ways, perhaps, these oaths would be as effective if they involved only a suitably solemn form of words. But the courts continue to bolster the words spoken by bringing out a book. If you open the book and try reading it in this situation the judge is likely to get rather grumpy. He will observe that you've missed the point. Although the oath wouldn't have quite the same gravitas if sworn on a copy of the latest John Grisham thriller, it's not the text of the book that makes the oath powerful so much as the cultural power ascribed to the book as an object. Barack Obama chose to say the oath of office at both of his inaugurations on a Bible that had belonged to Abraham Lincoln. The power of this book is twofold: the authority of the text it contains is bolstered by the volume's provenance. The US House of Representatives allows newly elected members to choose the book used to swear them in. It doesn't have to be a religious text. But there has to be a book: you can't be sworn in without one. The power of the book to signify the seriousness of the oath is more important than the contents of the book chosen.

❧

Book signings are another important event in the social life of books. There's a long history of authors inscribing copies of their books for friends. But the modern book signing, where authors sign books for a queue of fans, is a recent invention. Bestselling authors now sign thousands of copies, either at signing events or in advance. (I heard that Ian Rankin signed 30,000 copies of his latest novel.) I think this reveals something interesting about the life of books.

In order to grasp what's going on at a book signing, it might help to think about how looking at a painting in a gallery is different from looking at a novel in a library. When you're standing in front of a painting, you're looking at the actual object that the artist worked on – he had the same canvas in front of him in the studio, and he actually reached out his brush and made the very marks you see in the gallery. In certain circumstances, we might be happy enough to look at a reproduction, but we don't think it's interchangeable with the painting itself. The painting is the thing. The philosopher of aesthetics Nelson Goodman, whose ideas I'm borrowing here, calls painting an 'autographic' art, because the work of art is identical with the material object the artist worked on.[8]

The arts of writing don't exist in the same way. When you pick up a novel in a library – or a poem or play – you're not holding in your hand something that its creator actually touched. Where a painting is made from paint and canvas, a work of literature is made from words, which don't have a material existence of their own in the way that paint does. Our only access to a literary work is through paper and ink, but the work isn't made from those things. When you're thinking about a novel, you can draw a line between the object (paper, ink) and the artwork (words, ideas). It doesn't make sense to do that when you're thinking about a painting. Writing has a different mode of existence from painting. Goodman calls this kind of art, which has no physical substrate, 'allographic'.

When we queue up to get our copy signed at a book-signing, I think that – on some subconscious level – we've grasped something about the ontology of the book that Goodman's distinction illuminates. The author's signature acts as a kind of guarantee that this book is his or her work. It's not that we doubt that the author wrote the words. But, when the author signs the title page, the signature, like the signature on a painting, shows that this individual claims this object as their own production. This is why authors quite often cross out the printed version of their name when they sign. Their action negates the book's existence as a product of industry or commerce and reclaims it as the product of their own artistic effort. I've come to see book signings as rituals that attempt to convert allographic artworks into autographic ones. In the process, they make buying the book feel less like buying a machine-made product and more like buying a work of art.

This feeling is intensified when the book is not just inscribed by its author but actually inscribed *to you* as an individual. Bookshops often ask authors to sign a few extra copies that they can sell after the author has gone onto the next stop on his or her tour. But these never seem as satisfying as having the author write your name in the book as well as their own. Having a book inscribed to you – even if it's by an author that you've encountered only for a few minutes at a book-signing event – offers the comforting sense that this particular book is unlike any other copy of the same title. The book may be a mass-produced commodity, but the inscription allows you to imagine that this particular copy has been destined for you alone. You're more likely to read it attentively and keep it carefully as a result. The inscription allows us to turn a blind eye to the many other people besides the author who were involved in the production, marketing and selling of the book, as well as the many other purchasers and readers besides us who will consume it. Just for a moment, it seems less like a product and more like a gift, less like a public statement and more like a personal message. Signing the book is a way of adding value to it as an object.

Once I started to pay attention to books as objects in private and in public, I soon began to notice how many other objects we use alongside books. Books sit at the centre of a constellation of other objects, which orbit around the book like planets around the sun. Before long, I had a whole list of other items that are more or less related to books and reading: bookmarks, bookplates, book bags, reading spectacles, reading lights, reading chairs, and many more. Many of these things exist only because of books: they've been specially designed and manufactured to be used alongside books. Others are versions of everyday objects modified or repurposed to serve readers. Think of all the things that get used as bookmarks: postcards, business cards, train tickets, boarding passes, take-away menus. Charity-shop workers always have stories of the strange things they've found inside donated books, from antique cigarette cards to ten-pound notes. Thinking about the book as an object opens the door to a wider material culture of bookishness.

When I pick up a book to read, I find I often pick up something else as well – a bookmark, a pencil, a notepad, a cup of tea. The way that I use books is accompanied and supported by the ways in which I use other objects. There's a long history of this kind of connection between books and other things. For much of the history of the codex, its manufacturing process left the page edges on the front and top of the book as folds of paper (what bibliographers call the fore-edge and top-edge). In modern books these edges are trimmed with a mechanical guillotine to leave them smooth. In earlier ages, they might have been trimmed by bookbinders, but purchasers who wanted to read their books in wrappers, before they were bound, had to cut their way through them with knives, opening the leaves of the book as they went. Some probably cut one fold at a time and read the pages they had exposed before cutting the next leaf. A few might have cut open all the leaves of the book before they started reading. But most probably cut a few folds, read those pages, and then cut a few more. As a result, we can see whether these readers made it all the way through the book or not. For these readers, picking up a book often meant picking up a knife too.

Most well-off readers had special paper knives for opening books, which they might also have used for letters. In some cases, however, any knife that came to hand might be pressed into service. The nineteenth-century essayist Thomas De Quincey recounts how William Wordsworth took up a volume of Edmund Burke's writings while he was having tea with De Quincey and, finding the leaves unopened, grabbed a buttery knife from the tea table and used that to cut his way into his friend's book. De Quincey claimed not to mind, but he did mention that the knife 'left its greasy honours behind it upon every page' where they were visible 'to this day'.[9] A few years ago I bought a set of Benjamin Disraeli's novels that had obviously never been read. Although they were over seventy-five years old, the pages were unopened. I had to cut my way through them with a paper knife. In the process, I experienced a physical relationship with the book that was rather different from what I was used to, and must have been closer to that of readers in earlier centuries. When reading the books in bed, however, I did have an unfortunate tendency to leave the knife on top of the sheets when I turned out the light. Ever since, I've associated Disraeli's novels with unpleasant nocturnal surprises.

The objects that get drawn into the book's orbit help reveal how people use books and make them part of their lives. Women readers in the past often interspersed their reading with needlework. Both were socially acceptable activities that you could do sitting down at home, and both required good light, so they were often done in the same room, and even the same chair. Women who picked up their work basket full of scraps, needles and thread with one hand must often have picked up a book with the other. And sometimes the activities of reading and sewing got stitched together. Scripture reading might supply texts to be embroidered into a sampler.

And the work basket might provide tools for reading too. I recently looked at an eighteenth-century volume from the library of a Scottish country house: tucked between the pages was a pin, probably borrowed for a makeshift bookmark and forgotten. It had almost certainly been there for over two centuries, slowly rusting and leaving greenish stains on the adjacent leaves. In another volume from the same library the title page had started to fall out, and someone had pinned it back into the book, as though it were a patch on a pair of trousers.

Using books sometimes means not only patching them up, but also pulling them apart. Although modern librarians frown on this kind of thing, scholars in the sixteenth and seventeenth centuries often read with scissors or knives in hand, cutting up both manuscript and printed sources into scraps or slips and filing these slips according to categories in elaborate systems.[10] Readers of all kinds used pens and ink to write in their books. Before the invention of the modern pencil and the ballpoint pen, this was a much more involved practice than it is today, requiring a bottle of ink to dip your quill in and a penknife to 'mend' the nib.[11] Some readers even painted marginal illustrations into their books.[12] All these examples suggest how using books is often nothing like the disembodied communion between a reader's mind and an author's that Proust described. Instead, it's a thoroughly material business, involving a variety of tools and objects.

～～

Books have their own furniture too. Eighteenth-century gentlemen furnishing their libraries needed not only book-cases but also specially designed library chairs, tables and ladders. Lecterns made books available for reading aloud in public, for example in a lecture theatre, a church or a monas-tery (where books were often read aloud during meals), and also in families where scripture reading and family prayers might be routine events. Lecterns also make it possible to read books hands-free, while doing something else. With the help of a lectern, you can read and eat at the same time, for example, or consult a cookbook while making a recipe from it. In his sixties, the poet Philip Larkin put a lectern in his bedroom with a Bible on it; he reportedly read the book while shaving, which sounds like a dangerous habit. I'm not sure whether this mode of reading influenced his conclusion that the Bible was 'absolute balls'.[13]

Some people needed more specialised equipment. The book wheel was an early modern machine that allowed its user to mount several books onto trays on a large wheel. When the wheel was turned, the trays stayed upright, like the cars on a Ferris wheel. This allowed Renaissance scholars to consult several books one after another, comparing them against each other. Like toggling between windows on a computer desktop, spinning the book wheel was designed to let readers who needed to examine several texts at once move between them with minimum fuss.

As that analogy suggests, we have our own versions of these bookish objects today. The noise-cancelling headphones worn by a twenty-first-century worker on a commuter train serve the same purpose as the wing-backed armchair sitting in a Victorian parlour. Both create a semi-permeable zone of privacy in the middle of a space that has to be shared with other people. Both provide a kind of screen between the individual and those around them. And both, therefore, can be used to facilitate reading. Like the Victorian with his head in a book, shielded from sociability by the furniture, the modern commuter in her headphones, squinting at a novel on her phone, is making an environment that's inhospitable to reading more reader-friendly. The headphones clamped to her ears allow her to carve out time and space for reading in a busy, overstimulating environment.

My faulty copy of *Middlemarch* may not have let me finish George Eliot's novel, but it did get me thinking about books in a new way. They started to come into focus for me – as I hope they're now starting to come into focus for you – as objects in their own right, not only as containers of words. Once I started to pay attention to books as things, I realised that you couldn't talk about the book as an object without also talking about the different things that people did with books. Reading was one of those things, of course, and people's readings left their own traces on books. But reading was only one of the things that people did with books, and not always the most important. Reading is often thought of as something done in private, but books also had a public life, and they demanded to be understood in relation to the wider world. And people used books alongside other objects, so they couldn't be understood in isolation from the rest of the material culture of bookishness. I had been taught to ignore the book itself in favour of the text it contained, but once I stopped looking through it and started looking at it, its secret life was revealed.

CARAVAGGIO: *ST JEROME*

Caravaggio made several attempts to depict St Jerome, but as far as I'm concerned the most interesting is the one he painted in Rome around 1605. Jerome had translated the Bible into Latin, and the Catholic Church had officially endorsed his version at the Council of Trent around fifty years before Caravaggio painted this work. The saint was a popular subject for artists; he was usually painted with his red cardinal's hat and his emblem, the tame lion, sitting like a shaggy dog alongside Jerome as he worked surrounded by books in his study. In fact, Jerome was never a cardinal; the rank didn't exist until centuries after his death. I don't suppose he really had a tame lion either. In any case, Caravaggio leaves out the hat and the lion entirely and includes just three massive books on Jerome's simple, sturdy table, plunging the rest of the scene into the kind of deep shadow that was one of his trademarks.

Jerome is a study in physical decay. His body is so frail it almost disappears from the painting altogether. His lower half – associated with sex and excretion – vanishes behind a shapeless red drapery, the only remains of his cardinal's robe. Two glints of white paint stand out – the shine of Jerome's bald head, which reflects an impossible light, and the white quill pen, whose feathers have all been ripped off, clasped in the saint's frail hand. Almost all that's left of Jerome is a head to think and a pen to write. And even these won't last long, the painting seems to say. The saint's bony head and drapery to the right are balanced in the composition by the rumpled white tablecloth to the left and the skull on his desk. They are a reminder of what Jerome himself will become. The head full of intelligence and inspiration will, soon enough, become a skull emptied of its consciousness and wrapped in a winding sheet.

In this painting, the body perishes, but the book survives. Jerome's books are far more substantial and durable than he is. Huge folios containing hundreds of pages, they dominate the centre of the composition. While the saint is emaciated, the books in their leather bindings are sleek and solid. As well as being a meditation on mortality, this painting is a celebration of the book, and in particular the codex. We know that Christians were early adopters of the codex format, but the historical Jerome, who lived from 347 to 420 CE, finishing his translation in 384, probably worked with scrolls as much as with codices. The books that weigh down Jerome's table in Caravaggio's painting are therefore something of an anachronism. Caravaggio places the codex in the middle of his painting as a reminder that books allow our words to outlive us. The materiality of Jerome's books is reassuring – you can almost hear the dull thud they made when he put them down on the desk, almost feel the strain in the saint's wasted arms as he lifts and moves them. While the saint is heading towards the grave, the books are here to stay. Their heft is a metaphor for their importance – these are weighty books in two senses, both heavy and profound.

But for all the massive sturdiness of the books on Jerome's desk, they won't last forever. One of them is already starting to decay. The leather binding of the closed book to the left of the picture is beginning to peel away from the spine. The closed book might symbolise the faulty versions of the Bible that Jerome is superseding with his new translation, and the shabby binding could be an image of their obsolescence. But there's little difference between the three books in the painting. The book in which Jerome is apparently writing doesn't look any more splendid or solid than the others. At the same time as it sets the durability of the book against the fragility of the body, then, this painting also includes a reminder that even divinely inspired texts have to circulate in books that are physical objects, subject to wear and tear, and prone to decay.

Like many painters, Caravaggio put himself through an apprenticeship of still lifes. Many of his earlier paintings depict assemblages of flowers and fruit, including some in various stages of wilting and rotting. A skull – the traditional *memento mori* – is also a standard part of the still-life paraphernalia. These so-called *vanitas* paintings display both the abundance of God's creation and the transience of all earthly things. Everything is tending towards its own dissolution. Caravaggio brings the same sensibility to some of his depictions of human bodies, which are scrutinised for evidence of their mortality. Jerome's body is evidently, painfully mortal. He looks as though he hasn't got long left in this world, and the skull reinforces that impression. But, in this picture, Caravaggio turns the same searching gaze onto the book. On one hand Jerome's books are robust, massive, powerful. This painting offers a glimpse into the primal scene of a book that would change the world, becoming a key Christian text for centuries to come. And yet, Caravaggio cannot help but depict the books as subject to the common lot of objects as well as men – they too are part of the fallen world, and they too are subject to the ravages of time.

Caravaggio was at the height of his powers, in his mid thirties, when he painted this version of Jerome. He was a successful artist with wealthy patrons, including the powerful Cardinal Scipione Borghese, who might have commissioned this painting (which now hangs in the Galleria Borghese in Rome). But his wild life would soon catch up with him. Not long after he finished the picture he killed a man in a brawl over a gambling debt and was forced to flee Rome. We don't know whether he took any books with him when he left, but it seems unlikely he had room for the large and heavy folios from the painting of St Jerome in his luggage. It's perfectly possible that they still exist in a library somewhere, but it's more likely that – like most of the books ever produced – they've been lost to history. All that's left of them is their depiction on Caravaggio's canvas. There, Caravaggio seems to insist that, whatever else they are – ark of God's Word, source of divine light, key to salvation – they are also things.

3

BOOK/SELF

*How books shape our identities
and signal them to others*

always make a beeline for the bookcases. If, indeed, there are any. If you invite me into your house, sooner or later I'll sidle over to the bookshelf and, head cocked to one side, examine the books. You can tell a lot about people by the books they put on their shelves. Are there expensive hardbacks, or antiquarian volumes in leather bindings? Are there multi-volume sets of the complete works of standard authors? Books in foreign or classical languages? The rows of red or green Loeb bindings favoured by students of the classics? The old Penguins sought after by collectors? Is the coffee table weighed down with huge glossy art books that no one ever seems to open? Are there guidebooks from foreign travels, with tickets and receipts still tucked into the pages? Or are the shelves lined with paperback detective novels, their spines creased and their corners splayed? Has the bookshelf been stocked from antiquarian booksellers or from charity shops? Are the books there for use or for show? Is this person a hoarder who keeps every book they read, or a minimalist who maintains a scrupulously curated selection? And, perhaps most interestingly of all, what's missing from the shelves? Are there other books elsewhere in the house: self-help books mouldering in cardboard boxes in the attic, religious tracts piled in the study, volumes of erotica hidden in the bedroom? Or, finally, are all the books hidden from view – just a list of titles on an e-book reader?

It took a long time for bookshelves to take on their current form.[1] Medieval readers kept their books in chests or displayed them on lecterns. Books were expensive luxuries, so they tended to be either kept securely locked away or exhibited ostentatiously. When they were gathered together in numbers, it was often in institutions such as monasteries, rather than private collections. They tended to be kept lying flat on shelves. Some books had 'bosses' on the covers – little nodules of bone or nuggets of metal that served as feet when the book was lying flat, protecting the binding from shelf damage and allowing air to circulate around the book. Many medieval and early modern books don't have any markings on the spine, but the title or shelfmark has been written on the opposite side of the book, along the front edges of the pages. This reflects the fact that books were once shelved this way around, with the fore-edge facing out. In some libraries (such as the seventeenth-century one preserved intact at Hereford Cathedral), the books were stored upright, with the fore-edge outwards, and chained to the shelves for safekeeping. The books had to be secured because they were scarce and valuable items. But the modern bookshelf is a product of bibliographical abundance. We need bookshelves because books are now readily available and relatively affordable. And in those conditions an individual – even one of limited means and no particularly bookish temperament – can have his or her own shelf of books.

Your books reveal who you are. To display them where other people can see them is to exhibit a particular version of your self. Maybe you curate this version carefully, putting your 'best' books in the most visible places. Or maybe you stack your books up any which way – the bibliographical equivalent of going out in tracksuit bottoms without shaving. Either way, your books, like your clothes, your hairstyle, or your personal grooming, are sending messages about you. In fact, our books actually reveal more about us than our appearance, because they are visible markers of an inner life. Browsing through someone else's bookshelf is a strangely intimate experience. On display in their living room you can see something important about what they know and what they love. The books they choose to keep and display may be objects they've invested in emotionally, treasured possessions that call up memories of powerful reading experiences.

If you look closely, you can see what the books mean to their owner. Some of them have been read cursorily, leaving little sign of handling. Others have not been read at all. Still others reveal from the wrinkles in their paperback spines (or, in earlier ages, their uncut pages) that the reader gave up part-way through. As I scan along the shelves, I sometimes come across one book that bears the scars of long use. Richard Holmes, the biographer of Percy Shelley and Samuel Taylor Coleridge, describes the thrill he gets from seeing one of his books read to pieces in this way: 'Nothing is so moving to the biographer as finding an old copy of his book in a stranger's hands, battered and wine-stained from its voyages, its margins scrawled, its poetry underlined, its pages bent with maps and postcards, its cover bleached with sun and sea.'[2] Here is the heart of a person's private library, and when I've located it,

I feel as if I'm very close to the heart of the person him- or herself. These are the volumes that have become most tightly sutured into their owner's subjectivity. Their tattered condition is a testament to that fact, while the volumes themselves, standing on the bookshelves within easy reach, are the outward and visible sign of the hidden selfhood that treasures them, the inner life that they have helped to build.

Of course, not every house has its bookshelves. 'Bookishness' – in the sense of buying, reading, keeping and displaying books – is partly a matter of temperament, as well as one of wealth or class. Books, in fact, function as badges of identity precisely because not everyone has the same kind of access to them or the same level of interest in them. Spending time with books, and spending money on books, is a choice that signals to others that you are a certain kind of person. *I* read books; *you* watch television; *he* plays video games.

We can use books to define who we are – and who we are not. When I buy a book, or borrow one from a library, I'm making an implicit claim to be the kind of person who reads this kind of book, or perhaps I'm saying that I want to be that person. The book may be well within my reading comfort zone – the latest book by a familiar author, say, or the next instalment in a series. In this case it bolsters an identity that's already well established. Or it may be a risk, a stretch, an aspiration – a work recommended by a friend whose judgement I admire, or referred to in something else I've read, or reviewed favourably in the press or online. In that case it marks an effort to develop my identity and become someone that I am not, or not yet.

Selfhood is an ongoing project. If reading is, in part, an effort to shape who we will be in the future, then perhaps always wanting to read something new betrays some dissatisfaction with who we are now. And because printed books exist in many identical copies, the individuality they sponsor also relates to membership of the community of the book's other readers. Buying a book is joining a club – or at least proposing yourself for membership of one.

In his novel *The Unbearable Lightness of Being* (1984), Milan Kundera describes a character who, as a young woman, loved to walk down the street with a book under her arm. 'It had the same significance for her as an elegant cane for the dandy a century ago,' Kundera writes. 'It differentiated her from others.'[3] I remember people I knew as a teenager carrying books in this way. Dickens's massive novel *Bleak House* seemed to be a popular choice. For me it was Byron's comic epic poem

Don Juan. These books were ambitious undertakings for readers of our age. We carried the thick paperbacks around with
us for weeks as our bookmarks slowly edged towards the back
cover. Embarking on them was a declaration and finishing
them an achievement.

We wanted to be taken seriously. We wanted people to
know that we took *ourselves* seriously. The books, we hoped,
made clear that we weren't just casual readers but committed
students. We eyed the books of others, looking for like-minded
peers. In the same way, for Kundera's character, 'books were
the emblems of a secret brotherhood',[4] although I remember
spotting as many sisters as brothers. Some adolescents sig-
nalled their identity by sporting a football shirt in the colours
of their favourite team. Some fashioned a sense of self by wearing a leather jacket adorned with the names of their favourite
bands. And some accessorised their individuality with books,
carrying a copy of *Anna Karenina* so you knew what kind of
person you were dealing with. You can't do this with e-books
in the same way, because tablets and e-readers look the same
whatever you're reading on them. Teenagers of the future will
have to find another way to distinguish themselves when no
one carries a fat paperback under their arm any more.

I don't think any of my schoolfriends went on to become great heroes, conquerors or leaders of expeditions or military operations. Maybe it wasn't that kind of school. But by carrying our chosen books with us we were following in the footsteps of some 'great men'. Alexander the Great, according to Plutarch, always carried a volume of Homer with him on his military campaigns. The stories of gods and warriors in the Homeric epics inspired him as he pursued his own conquests. Napoleon was never without his copy of Ossian's poetry as he set about building his empire. It allowed him to imagine himself as a version of Ossian's mythical warrior hero, Fingal.

Ernest Shackleton carried a Bible on his expedition to Antarctica. It had been presented to him by Queen Alexandra (widow of King Edward VII) in 1914. When the crew had to abandon their ship, the *Endurance*, Shackleton insisted on leaving behind everything but necessities in order to lighten the loads they had to drag across the ice. He tore two pages out of Queen Alexandra's Bible and discarded the rest. One page contained the inscription from the queen. The other contained verses from the book of Job (38:29), which ask rhetorically, 'Out of whose womb came the ice? and the hoary frost of heaven, who hath gendered [i.e. engendered] it?'

For these ambitious men, books were a prop to wield, as well as a solace in difficult times. Their books functioned as talismans, taking on an importance beyond the texts they contained. I'm sure Shackleton had that verse from Job off by heart long before he tore the page out of his Bible. But sometimes it's not enough to read and recall the words in a book: we need to remember how important the book is for us by keeping a treasured copy close at hand. Or, in Shackleton's case, a fragment of one.

※

The connection between books and identities relies on the books we don't read (or at least those we aren't *seen* reading) as well as those we do. Twentieth-century commuters supposedly hid copies of *Lady Chatterley's Lover* behind their newspapers. Readers of erotica don't tend to leave their books lying around for the babysitter to find. If you're going for a job interview, make sure you haven't got a trashy novel sticking out of your bag – it might give the wrong impression. Don't turn up for dinner with your highbrow friends while clutching the wrong paperback.

In certain circumstances, it's prudent to pretend you've read something when you haven't – I suspect some of my students do this rather a lot. But on other occasions, people also pretend not to have read – or not to remember – books they almost certainly know something about. A few years ago, I was invited to dinner at high table in an Oxford college. This is either a perk of my job or an occupational hazard, depending on your perspective; I always enjoy it. On this occasion, I was introduced over sherry to a particularly self-satisfied young don in a velvet jacket, who wanted – for reasons I cannot now recall or, indeed, even imagine – to mention *Fifty Shades of Grey* in conversation. He couldn't bring himself to admit that he actually knew the title – that would have been far too lowbrow – and so a ridiculous little pantomime ensued. 'That book that everyone's made such a fuss about, you know the one,' he said, gesturing airily with the hand that wasn't clutching his sherry glass. '*Fifty* something-or-other.' He was hoping that I'd supply the title, and thus reveal that I paid much more attention to popular culture than he did. I was determined not to play along.

Usually in these situations, the more knowledge you can display about books the better. But here was a new refinement – showing off how little one knew about certain books turned out to be just as important as showing off how much one knew about others. And so, for what seemed like ages, we engaged in a curious game of competitive ignorance, as he pretended not to remember the title of the book, and I pretended I had no idea what he was talking about. It wasn't the prurient subject matter that was the problem. I'm sure his memory would have worked just fine if we'd been talking about the erotic poetry of Sappho or Catullus. It was snobbery, not prudery, that had left him tongue-tied. As an academic, his self-image was bound up with books, but it was shaped as much by the books he feigned ignorance of as by those he claimed to know well. Later on, I noticed him fussily making sure the guests all knew in which direction to pass the port.

Under certain circumstances, we want to distance ourselves not from any particular books but from books in general. Goethe's sentimental novel *The Sorrows of Young Werther* (1774) was a European bestseller. At the beginning of the novel, when Werther retreats to the country, his friend thinks he might want some books sent to him to keep him amused. But Werther has other plans for his rural retreat. 'You ask should you send me my books? – For heaven's sake, my dear friend, do no such thing!' Werther has had enough of books. 'I have no wish to be directed, encouraged, fired up, any more.'[5] He makes only one exception – his treasured copy of Homer, which (like Alexander the Great) he carries around with him.

In George Crabbe's poem *Peter Grimes* (1810), the young Peter refuses to sit and read the Bible with his poor but pious father in their cottage. He prefers to be outside than to spend his time with books. '"It is the word of life," the parent cried; / "This is the life itself," the boy replied' (lines 18–19). Crabbe's Grimes is not the sympathetic, tragic character that the composer Benjamin Britten and librettist Montagu Slater would make of him in their 1945 opera based on the poem. But his rejection of books in favour of 'life itself' in Crabbe's poem isn't meant as an early hint of the depravity that will reveal itself later, when Grimes causes the deaths of the apprentice boys in his care. Instead, the young Grimes's rejection of books just tells us that he's a youth of uncontrollable animal spirits, too boisterous to sit inside on a sunny day. Our identities are shaped not only by the books we buy, store, read and carry around with us but also by the books we set aside in favour of other things. For Grimes, as for Werther, living fully and living well means knowing when to turn your back on books.

In 1798 William Wordsworth made this point in a pair of poems called 'Expostulation and Reply' and 'The Tables Turned'. In the first, the speaker's friend chides him for spending too much time mooning about outside, and not enough with his books. 'Where are your books? – that light bequeathed / To Beings else forlorn and blind! / Up! up! and drink the spirit breathed / From dead men to their kind' (lines 5–8). To live without books, the friend argues, is to ignore your place in history, to fail to learn from the past, 'As if [. . .] none had lived before you!' (lines 11–12). But in the second poem, Wordsworth replies to this charge by asserting the claims of nature over those of books: 'Books! 'tis a dull and endless strife: / Come, hear the woodland linnet, / How sweet his music! on my life, / There's more of wisdom in it.' (lines 9–12). You're better off going for a walk and listening to the birds than staying indoors and pushing on through another chapter. Spending too much time with your books, as the young Grimes thought, is cutting yourself off from something important in life, not enriching your life.

It's no coincidence that all these examples – Goethe, Crabbe, Wordsworth – come from the period when printed books were starting to become much cheaper and more readily available. From about the 1770s onwards, the total number of books in circulation started to increase exponentially, marking a growth in book production that has barely slowed down since. This was the beginning of the age of print saturation. Printing technology advanced, with the first all-metal presses and the first machine-made paper. Books were distributed along much improved roads and shipping lanes, and soon along canals and railways too. And literacy rates went up thanks to improved education, helping to create a mass reading public.

By 1865, when the French poet Stéphane Mallarmé wrote 'La chair est triste, hélas! et j'ai lu tous les livres' ('Flesh is sad, alas! and I've read all the books'), there were in fact far too many books for anyone to read them all. He was not stating a literal fact (unless he meant 'all the books on my shelf') but evoking a generalised sense of ennui. For people growing up in this period, books seemed to be available in numbers that would have been unknown to their grandparents. In these circumstances, literary writers like Goethe, Crabbe and Wordsworth sometimes felt conflicted about books. On one hand they disdained nerdy absorption in books in favour of healthy encounters with nature. On the other hand, they relied on the book market to circulate their works. Some of our ambivalence about books is inherited from Goethe, Crabbe and Wordsworth. Sometimes we feel as if we've had enough of books, and we want to get away from them altogether. But this reaction is actually an oblique testament to the power of books to shape our identities, and the fact that they pervade our sense of ourselves to such a large extent.

Perhaps it's because books can take possession of our consciousness so powerfully that we, in turn, take possession of them so forcefully. As I mentioned before, there's a long history of people marking their ownership of books, with bookplates, stamps or inscriptions on the endpapers. Children often take possession of their books in this way, writing their names in the front to protect their books from being appropriated by siblings or classmates. This can be especially important when everyone in the class is using the same textbook or the same reading primer. The ownership inscription serves a practical purpose: like a name-tag sewn into a school uniform, it tells us whose book this is when there might be several like it. In shared childhood bedrooms, ownership inscriptions stake claims to territory. When adults mark their ownership of books, I think, they're following a similar logic. The handwritten name or pasted-in bookplate allows books that have been lent to find their way back to their owners. But it also performs a more fundamental act of appropriation. The ownership inscription insists that, of all the copies of this book that are in circulation, this one is special. This one is *mine*.

An inscription separates the book from the rest of the print run and individualises it. It customises it for a particular reader. But it also serves to attach it to another set of books

– those in my library. While there are usually no other copies of this *title* marked with my signature, stamp or bookplate, there are lots of other *books* in which I have declared my ownership in the same way. The mark of ownership, therefore, connects this book with all the others that I have marked in a similar fashion. It declares that this particular copy has taken up its place in my reading life, and among my possessions. Declaring the identity of the owner on the endpapers of the book is also a way of recognising the importance of books in shaping that identity.

Since Alexander the Great brandished his copy of Homer on the military campaign trail, books have been indispensable props for a certain kind of self-fashioning. Portraits often depict their sitters clutching books. They may actually be absorbed in reading a book – showing someone reading has often been a shorthand for art's aspirations to capture the inner life, as in Chardin's 1734 depiction of a well-dressed reader absorbed in a large folio while his quill pen stands ready at his elbow for making notes, or Vermeer's painting from the 1650s of a woman reading a letter at a window. Or the sitter may have one finger between the pages, marking their place, as though they've just looked up from their reading for a moment – in this case the interrupted book reinforces the illusion that a painting that took hours to produce nonetheless depicts an instant in its subject's life. Deploying a book as a prop also shows that the sitter has something more important to do than sit for their portrait – it suggests that the portrait is not a record of their vanity but something executed while they passed their time productively in reading. I don't suppose anyone will ever ask to paint my portrait, but if they do I certainly plan to take a book along to the sittings. I'll choose a cracking detective story to pass the time, and then get the artist to paint 'Homer' or 'Milton' on the front cover afterwards.

Whether they are read or not, books have also provided a conventional backdrop for staging erudition and power. Many lawyers' offices are still lined with volumes of legal proceedings, even though the physical books have long since been superseded by searchable databases. The uniform spines ranged along the shelves are a parade of professional knowledge, designed to reassure clients that the lawyer knows his or her business and is worth the fee. Universities often decorate their walls with portraits of senior administrators, who almost invariably pose in front of bookshelves, even if their working lives are actually filled with meetings, memos and emails, leaving little time for reading books. The books are there to signify that knowledge is their business. This is nothing new: in 1805, the poet, author and editor Robert Southey complained in a letter that 'books are now so dear that they are becoming rather articles of fashionable furniture more than anything else'.[6]

In Jules Verne's classic tale of adventure, *Twenty Thousand Leagues Under the Sea* (1869), Captain Nemo renounces human society to live on his fantastic submarine, the *Nautilus*. But he takes some of the comforts of civilisation with him, including a library of 12,000 uniformly bound volumes in several languages. The narrator, Professor Aronnax, proclaims, 'I am absolutely astounded when I consider that it can follow you to the bottom of the seas.' Nemo delights in a 'library which would do honour to more than one of the continental palaces'.[7] In a story full of wonders, the existence of a submarine library is one of the most implausible. But the books are there to make a point. Verne uses the well-appointed library to send a clear sign that Nemo is a highly civilised man, despite his misanthropy. The books tell the reader exactly who Nemo thinks he is.

A couple of years ago, I got a glimpse into another palace library, albeit one on dry land. The *Telegraph* printed a photograph of the Queen welcoming the Governor General of Canada into the library at Balmoral, her Scottish residence.[8] Comparisons with a photo taken in the same room in the 1970s revealed that the books on the shelves hadn't moved in the intervening forty years. Now, this doesn't necessarily mean that they haven't been touched in that time. Perhaps the Queen regularly takes down a volume of Sir William Fraser's series on the chiefs of the Scottish clans (one of the works visible in the bookcase) when she fancies a bit of light reading, and puts it back on the shelf in the same place afterwards. But it seems more likely that for the last forty years – and perhaps much longer – the books have been standing guard in their serried ranks untroubled by any disturbances apart from regular dusting. I rather doubt anyone has ever read them.

They serve their purpose nonetheless, providing a backdrop to civilised life and a suitable stage set for hosting visiting dignitaries. In this case, the identity being shaped by these book-objects is not that of a private citizen but that of a public figure – a visible interest in Scottish clans might be taken as a mark of commitment to Scotland as part of a United Kingdom, for example, not just a sign of personal interest. The library is an in-between space, both private and public. Welcoming a visitor into a room where – at least in theory – she might relax in the evening with a good book, the Queen performs hospitality, suggesting that the Governor General merits not just the courtesy of a formal meeting in a state venue but the honour of an invitation into her home.

In these examples, the book as reading matter is irrelevant, and the book as object is everything. In fact, in these kinds of situation it's quite possible to use books that can't be read at all. Alexander Pope's 1731 poem 'Epistle to Burlington' includes a description of a library in a well-appointed country house where the books on the upper shelves are made of wood. Pope clearly thinks this fact reveals the owner as a philistine. Southey would have agreed: in the letter I just quoted, he complains about a nouveau-riche 'Wiltshire clothier who gives his bookseller no other instructions than the dimensions of his shelves'. Lots of cafes and pubs today do the same thing, buying books by the yard to decorate their walls. I was in one the other day that had a little sign saying 'books are for decoration only', just in case someone was tempted to try reading them.

Using fake books actually seems to have been quite common, even in some great libraries, where the book's potential as a tool for interior decoration outstripped its interest as an object for reading. The library at Chatsworth – home of the Dukes of Devonshire and one of England's greatest stately homes – includes doors covered with painted books that conceal the stairs to the library gallery. They have comic titles that give the game away. Some of these were suggested by the poet Thomas Hood, a friend of the 6th Duke of Devonshire, in the 1800s. When another door was added in the 1960s, the Duchess of Devonshire approached her friend Patrick Leigh Fermor (who made a brief appearance in the last chapter), asking him to come up with some more joke titles. His suggestions included *Intuition* by 'Ivor Hunch', and *Consenting Adults* by 'Abel N. Willing'.[9]

Pressing books into service as backdrops, or interior-design elements, can seem like a rather shabby practice. These might seem like bad ways to use books, as though there's something morally wrong about them, or just that they miss the point. Isn't the purpose of a book to be read, after all? Isn't it being turned aside from that purpose and prevented from fulfilling it when it's used for interior design, or display, or as a backdrop or a prop? No doubt when Sir William Fraser composed his volumes on the chiefs of Scottish clans he hoped that someone would read them, not use them as an expensive substitute for wallpaper or a brick in a diplomatic facade. But reading them is only one of the things we do with books, and not always the most significant. For a book to signal something about you, you don't necessarily need to have read it.

Books don't just signal our identities, though; they also help to constitute them. Books are a powerful mnemonic technology. Hamlet, charged by his father's ghost to avenge his father's death, promises to forget 'all saws of books' (that is, all the wise sayings he's learned from books), so that the ghost's 'commandment all alone shall live / Within the book and volume of my brain, / Unmixed with baser matter' (*Hamlet*, I.v.109–11). His brain hasn't just been stored with things he's read in books; it is itself a kind of book.

Remembering things and keeping track of things were some of the first uses for books and writing. Some of the earliest objects that we can recognise as books were created for this purpose. About 5,000 years ago in the Peruvian Andes, inhabitants of the first known civilisation in the Americas used knotted cords to keep accounts.[10] The cords were dyed different colours and then knotted in a system of strings hanging down from another, horizontal, string, a bit like the strings of fairy lights that hang from the eaves of suburban houses at Christmas. These knotted cords are called quipus (meaning 'knot' in the Quechua language of Peru) and they are some of the first 'books'.

Some quipus had only a few knotted strings, while others had as many as 2,000 cords. By knotting and reknotting the cords, quipucamayocs (people who specialised in making and maintaining quipus) could record transactions, keep inventories of goods and – perhaps – encode other kinds of information. The knots weren't a private code but one that could be read by any skilled quipucamayoc. Quipus were still in use when the Spanish conquistadors arrived in the 1530s. When quipus made their way back to Europe on colonisers' ships, scholars became fascinated by the idea that these exotic objects revealed a writing system utterly different from their own. They argued that the knots functioned like syllables and could be combined to represent words, make ideas visible and weave stories into being.[11] Modern specialists are more sceptical. They disagree about whether the quipus could represent words, place names or narratives, or whether they were more like spreadsheets used for accounting, storing only numerical information. But in any case, they seem to have relied on the interplay of the knotted cords and the memory of their users, whether they were remembering inventories of livestock or episodes in epic poems.

The modern printed codex is also a tool for creating and assisting memories. It marries a linear presentation of information to a spatial arrangement of it. In one respect, we encounter books in a linear fashion, the words unspooling in our consciousness as our eyes scan from left to right and from the top to the bottom of the page (if we're reading in a European language). In this respect, we receive the words on the page in much the same way as we would if we heard someone else reading them aloud, in person or on a recording. Considered like this, the book is a kind of external memory device in the sense that we can return to it again and 'hear' in our heads the same words in the same order.

But there's more to the connection between books and memory than this, I think. Each word occupies a particular place on the page in relation to other words and to blank spaces such as indents, paragraph breaks and margins. Each page, meanwhile, has its own particular place in the book. This spatial dimension to the book is essential to the way we perceive it and to how we remember what we read. We also orient ourselves in a tactile fashion. Jane Austen drew attention to this dimension of the book in the final chapter of *Northanger Abbey*, where she archly points out that there's not much point in a novelist trying to create suspense when the reader, expecting a happy ending, 'will see in the tell-tale compression of the pages before them, that we are all hastening together to perfect felicity'.[12] We can feel in our fingers how many pages have been read and how many are still to go.

In the late nineteenth century, the French ophthalmologist Louis Émile Javal observed that when people read, their eyes don't move smoothly from left to right and from top to bottom; they flick backwards as well as forwards, moving jerkily several times a second in little jumps that he called 'saccades'.[13] (To do something par saccades is to do it by fits and starts.) Scientists using eye-tracking software have confirmed Javal's observation. As we read we orient ourselves in relation to the architecture of the page. Concrete poetry makes maximal use of this fact, incorporating the spatial arrangement of words into the artistry of the poem. But there's a spatial dimension to any printed or manuscript book.

These facts can help us understand how books weave themselves into our memories. When I remember a particular moment in a book – a quotable passage, a key insight or a climactic scene – I often recall the words imperfectly. But I also often have a spatial and tactile sense of where those words appeared in the book – at the top or bottom of a page, on the left or right as I held the book, and so on. With some books the material construction of the book helps as well: the binding cracks or softens where I've put most stress on it, so that the book falls open to a passage that I've lingered over or returned to repeatedly. This is one reason why I always find it easier to locate favourite passages in my own copy of a book than someone else's.

❧

Part of the reason printed books work well as mnemonic devices, I suspect, is that they allow us to recruit two different processes of memory and yoke them together. Scientists distinguish between how our brains store and process auditory or phonological memories and how they deal with visual and spatial memories. So, if you're trying to remember a poem to recite you use one type of memory; but if you're trying to remember the route to your friend's house you use another. We understand the visual-spatial aspects of memory much better than the auditory or phonological aspects. This is partly because they are easier to explore experimentally. You can test a lab rat's visual-spatial memory by getting it to navigate a maze, but you can't ask a rat to memorise a poem. We know that visual-spatial memories seem to be stored in dedicated parts of the brain, and that we have a larger capacity for this kind of memory than for some other kinds of memory.

'Memory athletes' train themselves to memorise large amounts of information, such as the order of a pack of cards. They often use a 'location' method, such as a 'memory palace'. This technique associates things to be remembered with places in a space that you know well. For example, if you want to memorise a speech, you might associate each point you have to make with part of the auditorium where you'll be speaking, and then look at each of those points in turn as you speak. The reason this technique works so well is that it recruits the processes of visual-spatial memory, with their larger neural resources, to support the processes of verbal memory. When the two processes work alongside one another, we can remember verbal or numerical information much better than when we use auditory or phonological memory alone.

I suspect these two memory processes are also yoked together by the material form of the book. As you read a book, you lay down verbal memories of the words you've read. Striking lines of poetry, stately passages of prose or startling statistics will stick with you. But your memory of them will often be imperfect. Without going back to it, and reinforcing our memory, much of what we read slips away alarmingly rapidly. When you try to find a half-remembered passage again, however, you can also draw on all the visual-spatial cues you picked up from the book while you were reading. As well as remembering an interesting thought, pithily formulated, you might also recall that it occurred in the last paragraph of the introduction, or towards the beginning of the book's final chapter. You might have a visual memory of reading it at the bottom of a left-hand page, or the top of a right-hand one. These non-verbal cues can support your verbal memory, allowing you to find again a passage that you can recall only imperfectly.

If this is true then it suggests one important way in which paper books are different from e-books or audio books. Audio books and e-books don't contain visual-spatial or tactile clues in the same way as paper books. Although there haven't been very wide studies yet, there is some preliminary evidence that people reading on screens recall what they have read less thoroughly and effectively than people reading paper books.[14] The reason may have to do with the distinctive way that the printed codex supports processes of memory, in ways that we often take for granted.

When I look along my shelves, I'm also looking back at my past experiences, my past selves. On one bookshelf, I can see books relating to the subject of my PhD. On another, the long line of P. G. Wodehouse's novels that I've read since discovering his works a few years ago fills a shelf of its own. Some people keep their childhood favourites or buy new copies of them later in life. Ranging the books along the shelves like this – whatever order you put them in – is a way of turning time into space. Each book took hours to read, a whole shelf of them might have taken years to acquire, but standing alongside one another on the shelves, you can see them at a glance. Experience is spatialised, time flattened out.

My bookshelves thus offer the comforting sensation that reading is cumulative: that when I'm reading, I'm not just spending time with a book, but investing time in cultivating a more learned version of myself. As the bookshelves fill, so the reader's knowledge and range of reference accumulates. While a text offers an experience to be had over a few hours, a book is a possession that can be retained for years.

Buying, keeping, storing, arranging and displaying books are all ways of affirming that our concern with them endures. Some books – even if we first made their acquaintance in a library – seem to demand a more substantial commitment of both time and money. These ones we buy and keep. By doing so, we act on the hunch that we'll need them in the longer term. We don't just want them for the time it takes to read them; we imagine ourselves revisiting them in the future, whether it's to reread them from cover to cover, or just to dip into for a few pages, or to look up a favourite passage or a piece of information. Even if we can't recall most of what we've read, the presence of the books serves as an aide-memoire, a reassuring sign that not everything we've read is lost. Books on the shelves are sandbags stacked against the floodwaters of forgetting.

4

BOOK/RELATIONSHIP

How books form our relationships
with other people

When I was working as a professor's assistant, he and I used to lend each other books. I always felt a bit self-conscious about the sophomoric scribbles in the margins of the books I lent him. But one day when he returned a book to me, I was dismayed to discover that he'd added his own annotations. Once I got over my initial reaction – how dare he write in my book! – I noticed that his neat notes were not like the scrawls I'd seen in the margins of his own books. He wasn't jotting his thoughts down as he read through force of habit – he was making an effort to write legibly. His notes were messages to me, not reminders for him. They were an invitation to discussion. Together, we made that book into a space where we could start a three-way debate between ourselves and the author. The colloquy started in the pages of the book but spilled out of its covers and into our conversations. In the process, the book – and the way we used it – deepened and enriched our intellectual relationship.

Turning the pages of that volume, I discovered how books can become important to our relationships. If I hadn't thought much about this before, perhaps it's because we often imagine reading books as a solitary activity, an isolated and isolating experience. The relationships books seem to enable are relationships between the reader and the characters, not between the reader and other people. These relationships can be intensely emotional, as we see ourselves in the characters, or find ourselves falling a little in love with them, or discover that we love to hate them. And if the author writes in some version of his or her own voice, then we may feel a range of emotions towards the author too, from a deep emotional connection to book-hurling irritation. Books might interrupt or displace our relationships with other people, but they compensate us for this by creating new imaginary relationships while we read.

But do books really take us away from other people, substituting imaginary relationships for real ones? Is time spent among books always time stolen from social life and social responsibilities? I don't think that's the whole story. When I thought about it, I realised that my professor was only the latest in a long line of people to whom I had related, partly, through books. Books can help to shape relationships, from our most professional to our most intimate. Early on, books insinuate themselves between children and parents, when we sit together over the same book reading before bedtime. Later, books pass as tokens among people, leaving trails in their wake. We don't just use books to relate to authors and characters; we also use them to relate to one another. They get in among people, creating bridges or barriers between them. Books bring us together and, sometimes, they keep us apart.

Some people go further than my professor and I did, not just writing in their books but making them into the basis of elaborate shared projects. Historically, those who could afford to sometimes had their books bound in bespoke bindings emblazoned with their monogram, coat of arms or other insignia. Others liked to add illustrations to their books, buying engravings and having them inserted between the pages of the book when it was rebound. This was called extra-illustrating or 'Grangerising', because James Granger's *Biographical History of England* (1769) was one of the most popular books to embellish in this way. Once you started adding illustrations to a book, it was hard to know when to stop. Every person mentioned seemed to need a portrait, every location a landscape. And once you'd found a portrait of some interesting person to include, why not a picture of his wife as well, or his daughters, or his house? Some readers collected thousands of images, swelling their books to many volumes in the process. In Bolton Central Library, in Lancashire, you can see a Bible extra-illustrated at the end of the eighteenth century by the artist and publisher Robert Bowyer with some seven thousand engravings. In the process, Bowyer's Bible grew to forty-five giant volumes, which he housed in a specially commissioned bookcase.

But the granddaddy of all extra-illustrated books must be the so-called Sutherland Clarendon, now weighing down the shelves at the Ashmolean Museum in Oxford. This book reflects a relationship built on a shared obsession. The husband-and-wife team of Alexander and Charlotte Sutherland spent nearly forty-five years between them collecting images to illustrate their copy of Lord Clarendon's *History of the Rebellion* (first published in 1702). Alexander probably began collecting before he married Charlotte, his second wife, in 1812, but the project soon became a joint effort. Their enthusiasm rapidly outgrew Clarendon's history and extended to two more books by him, as well as Gilbert Burnet's *History of His Own Time* (1724). They had these books disbound and the pages inlaid into large sheets of paper, to allow for more and bigger illustrations. The project still wasn't finished when Alexander died in 1820, and Charlotte (who was almost thirty years younger than her husband) carried on collecting illustrations for another twenty years. When the books were finally finished in 1839 (whatever 'finished' might mean in these circumstances), they required sixty-one enormous volumes to accommodate almost 20,000 illustrations.[1]

The Sutherlands had embellished their books in a grand style, 'improving' them in the way that some eighteenth-century landowners improved their house and estate. In the process, they became as much the authors of the book as its original writers had been. The books gave them a shared project to work on as husband and wife, and although Sutherland wasn't an aristocrat, having made a fortune as a merchant, it provided the kind of cultivated leisure activity that seemed fitting for educated gentry. The project also connected them to a network of friends and acquaintances who helped them track down and buy the engravings. They sustained the effort over decades partly because it had become central to their marriage. It was such a giant undertaking, consuming so much of their energy, that I imagine they must sometimes have wondered privately what else they had in common besides their work on the book. After Alexander's death, illustrating the book also became a way for Charlotte to mourn his passing. Collecting and organising illustrations had been one of the things she spent most time doing with her husband while he was alive. Now that he was dead, perhaps expanding and sorting out the collection provided a way to honour his memory and to feel close to him.

⁓

The Sutherlands and other Grangerisers seem eccentric to us today. There's something obsessive in their drive to hoard images between the pages of their books. But lots of people still personalise their books, and in doing so shape or create relationships with other people. Joseph Conrad's son Borys enjoyed his father's novels so much that he took the latest one with him when, at the age of nineteen, he went to fight in the First World War. The book – *The Shadow Line* (1917) – was a seafaring tale about a young man assuming the captaincy of a ship bound for the Orient. It's a story about developing into maturity that has often been read as a metaphor for the First World War, and Conrad dedicated it to Borys 'and all others who like himself have crossed in early youth the shadow line of their generation'. Borys was wounded, but he survived his time at the front. The book didn't. His father gave him a new copy, and wrote above the dedication: 'To my dearest Boy to replace his own 1st edition copy lost in March 1918 on the Somme front notwithstanding his efforts to save it from the fire.'

The Shadow Line was Borys's favourite among his father's books, and he continued to reread it throughout his life.[2] But Conrad could be a prickly and distant father at times, and their relationship was sometimes strained. This inscription begins tenderly enough, naming Borys 'my dearest Boy'. But it's not all sweetness and light. Conrad includes a barely perceptible reminder that it was not just any copy that was lost, but a valuable first edition. And when he refers to his son's 'efforts to save it from the fire', Conrad seems to reassure himself that Borys really valued the lost book, and didn't let it go lightly – or to reassure Borys that he knows these things. This marked-up book therefore mediates between father and son in a way that shores up their relationship, and records Conrad's gratitude for his son's safe return from the front. But it cannot help but register submerged tensions between them at the same time.

Books connect people even more powerfully when those people are lovers – or when they would like to be lovers. Paolo and Francesca, in Dante's *Inferno*, were brought together by a book. Dante encounters them in the second circle of Hell, where the lustful are punished. Francesca explains how their affair began not long after she was married to Paolo's older brother. They were reading together in the garden, their heads bowing close to one another as they gazed at the same book. It was a story of chivalry, telling of how the knight Lancelot fell in love. When the story reached a climactic moment, and Lancelot finally kissed the woman he had so long yearned for, Paolo also kissed Francesca, all atremble (*'tutto tremante'*), and they found themselves in their own story of forbidden desire. Francesca comments coyly, 'we read no more that day' (*'quel giorno più non vi leggemmo avante'*).[3] The book becomes their pander – their go-between – turning a chaste relationship into a carnal one.

The dying John Keats made a printed book annotated with pencil marks into a token of love. In June 1820, before Keats left for Italy in search of a milder climate to strengthen his failing health, his lover Fanny Brawne gave him a ring and some flowers. In return, he spent some of his last days in

England marking 'the most beautiful passages' in a volume of Edmund Spenser's poetry that he sent to her.[4] It would be his last gift to her. Keats was not unusual in this respect. Many courting couples in the nineteenth century – as well as some today – read poems aloud to one another, making the book into a ligament of their relationship, a bond between them.

Poems and stories about love work best for this purpose, I suppose. The emotions represented in the book can easily become the emotions its readers feel for one another. But the physical form of the book plays its part in these encounters, too. In the right circumstances, even rather unromantic books can carry an erotic charge. Students getting together to study, for example, might find their attention straying from their textbook to their study partner. Heads bend together over the open book, like Paolo's and Francesca's, hands touch as pages turn, and desire can start to ignite. Or, when the lovers are separated by force of circumstance, like John Keats and Fanny Brawne, a book can provide a material connection between them, as though its pages carried the trace of one lover's touch to the other across the distance that separates them.

In a scene from Edward Bulwer-Lytton's 1828 novel *Pelham*, the conversation dwells briefly on the poetry of Felicia Hemans. Ellen, who will marry Henry Pelham at the end of the novel, expresses her delight at the volume of Hemans another character has idly picked up, and admits that the marks in the margins are hers. Shortly afterwards Pelham takes his leave. 'I seized my hat and departed – but not utterly alone – I had managed to secrete the book which Ellen's hand had marked.' The purloined book is a substitute for Ellen herself that saves Pelham from being 'utterly alone'. It offers access to her mind and her tastes, as well as the trace of her body in the marks made by her hand. '[T]hrough many a bitter day and sleepless night,' Pelham continues melodramatically, 'that book has been my only companion; I have it before me now, and it is open at a page which is yet blistered with the traces of former tears.'[5] Pelham's body leaves its own traces on the book, not in ink but in tears, and when they 'blister' the pages they reinforce the equation between touching the pages of the book and touching the skin of its owner.

In Pisa in 1819, Lord Byron borrowed a book from his lover Teresa Guiccioli and sat in her garden to read it. It was a copy of *Corinne*, by the exiled French author Madame de Staël, whom Byron had known in England and in Switzerland a few years before. Turning to the back of the book, he wrote on a blank space:

> My dear Teresa, – I have read this book in your garden; – my love, you were absent, or else I could not have read it. It is a favourite book of yours, and the writer was a friend of mine. You will not understand these English words, and *others* will not understand them – which is the reason I have not scrawled them in Italian. But you will recognise the handwriting of him who passionately loved you, and you will divine that, over a book which was yours, he could think only of love.[6]

The book becomes a container for a secret message to its owner, one that *others* – including, presumably, her husband – will not understand. Indeed, the addressee of the message won't understand it either, but, Byron says, she will 'divine' that it is a love note. The book has functioned as an aide-memoire, conjuring up amorous thoughts of Teresa in her absence, and now it becomes a go-between, carrying a message between the lovers. Working at the interface of English and Italian, of private and public, of licit and illicit communication, this book brings the lovers together while they are apart. By writing in Teresa's book, Byron also lays claim to it and, by extension, to her. It is now his book as well, just as she is now his. And, while it might be nearly identical to many other copies of *Corinne*, this one is marked out by Byron's inscription and made into a memorial of a particular afternoon, a peaceful place and a passionate love.

One of the first gifts I gave my wife was a copy of Lord Byron's poems – I was writing my doctoral thesis on Byron at the time, and I wanted her to share my enthusiasm for his poetry. I'm not sure, to be honest, if she ever read that book, but it's still on our shelves. In the years since that first gift, a number of other books have passed between us. Some of them have been presents on birthdays, anniversaries or Christmases. Others have been books that one of us has read and passed on to the other. Some of them have been books we know the other would enjoy, but which we don't think we'd like ourselves. Others have been books we've loved, and that we want the other person to love too. One of the things that's changed since my wife got a Kindle is that I have to ask her what she's reading, instead of seeing the book lying around the house. Over more than a decade of marriage, the giving and receiving of books has been a way for us to grow together, to explore the differences between us ('I can't believe you didn't like that book'), and to nudge our sensibilities closer together, one book at a time. We didn't fall in love over a book like Paolo and Francesca, but books have been an important part of our love affair too.

～～～

You don't have to enjoy or admire a book to use it in this way. The poet Philip Larkin and his lover Monica Jones shared a copy of Iris Murdoch's novel *The Flight from the Enchanter* (1956), which they systematically defaced. Passing the book back and forth between them over several years, they underlined phrases that struck them as sexually suggestive, even though they weren't meant to be ('Today it seemed likely to be especially hard'). They altered the text throughout, making it into a 300-page screed of childishly scatological and bawdy sexual humour. Not a single page escaped unmarked. 'Her lips were parted' became 'her legs were parted' and so on. Even the chapter headings and the list of other books by the same author at the front of the book were subjected to the same treatment. The rewritten novel was renamed 'The Shite from the Non-Enchanter'. In this curious process of defacement, the book became a shared secret, a place to let off steam, a way of uniting the lovers both in their distaste for Murdoch's prose and their collaborative ribaldry. 'For all the crudity and silliness of their alterations,' Larkin's biographer

Andrew Motion notes, 'they show a touching complicity.'[7] Trashing the book was another way of strengthening their relationship with each other.

Perhaps I should mention, though, that sharing books in this way doesn't guarantee a happy ending. The couple that reads together doesn't necessarily stay together. The British Library in London holds a book of hours produced in about 1500 that once belonged to Anne Boleyn. At the foot of one of the pages, Anne wrote, 'Be daly prove you shalle me fynde to be to you bothe lovynge and kynde' ('By daily proof, you shall find me to be both loving and kind to you'). Later in the book, her husband Henry VIII wrote (in French) 'If you remember my love in your prayers as strongly as I adore you, I shall hardly be forgotten, for I am yours. Henry R. forever.'[8] This touching pledge of devotion, written in the margins of a book that was in Anne's hands daily, turned out to be worth rather less than the parchment it was written on. Their marriage would last only three years before Henry had Anne arrested, tried for high treason and beheaded.

If books can bring us together, they can also keep us apart. Bring out a novel on the bus or in a cafe and it's a clear sign that you don't want other people to talk to you. Books can screen us off from other family members even when they're in the same room, creating bubbles of privacy in shared domestic spaces. And don't try snuggling up to your partner in bed when he or she is just getting to the last pages of a murder mystery. Not even the most ardent lover is more interesting than finding out whodunnit. Just as relationships can blossom through sharing and exchanging books, they can also wilt as a result of books borrowed and not returned, books gifted but never read, books loved by one person and hated by another. Philip Larkin's relationship with Kingsley Amis went through a rocky patch after Larkin lent Amis one of his favourite novels – Christopher Isherwood's *All the Conspirators* – and Amis hung onto it for far too long. Larkin resorted first to a series of vulgar capitalised postscripts ('SEND ALL THE CONSPIRATORS YOU FLARING BALLOCK YOU') and then to telling Amis 'seriously', 'that book is a book I value highly; I read it on an average once a month. Due to you I have been deprived of it for nearly 5 months. I want it!! Understand?'[9]

The relationships that books enable aren't always happy ones. Among collectors of books, highly prized volumes can lead to bitter rivalries. Walter Benjamin, a keen collector, wrote about the excitement of bidding for books at auctions. On one occasion, he recalled, another bidder seemed determined to outbid him for every lot he hoped to acquire. The mysterious gentleman was apparently prepared to go to any lengths to top Benjamin's bids, pushing up the prices of the books. They seemed locked into a rivalry that threatened to bankrupt them both. Benjamin was starting to resign himself to leaving the auction empty-handed, but there was one book still to come under the gavel that he particularly wanted. As the auctioneer announced this book, Benjamin had a moment of inspiration. If every bid from him just produced a higher bid from the other man, then he must not bid at all. He sat on his hands, praying that no one else would buy the book he coveted. The gamble paid off: no one bid on the book and it was set aside. A few days later, Benjamin went back to the auction house and bought the book from its second-hand department, paying a fraction of the price he would have paid at the sale.[10]

Benjamin's rival was an anonymous figure, unknown to him personally. But rivalries can also lead to lasting relationships. Thomas Dibdin, a bibliophile and author, had written a swooning account of the library of John Ker, 3rd Duke of Roxburghe, in his 1809 book *Bibliomania*. The centrepiece of the collection was a first edition of Boccaccio's *Decameron*, which at that time was thought to be the only surviving copy. When Roxburghe's library came to be sold in 1812, every serious book collector in England attended the auction, and expectations ran high. The *Decameron* caused a bidding war and sold for £2,260 – a record price that wouldn't be exceeded for the next fifty years. Dibdin hosted a dinner on the eve of the sale for those who planned to bid on the books, which became the founding event of the Roxburghe Club – the oldest and most distinguished society of bibliophiles. The Roxburghe Club was soon joined by other similar societies, such as the Ballantyne Club, which was founded in 1823 in Edinburgh. In these clubs, books brought men of a certain class together.

Reading together, like Paolo and Francesca or John Keats and Fanny Brawne, is only one way to enjoy a relationship mediated by books. As Dibdin understood, bibliographic sociability takes many forms. Book buying, owning and collecting can create and sustain social bonds. Over the last few years, I've been to lots of book fairs in different towns and cities, where second-hand and antiquarian book dealers gather to display their books. These days, the dealers all list their stock online, so you don't really need to go to a book fair to find a book to buy. But it's a fun thing to do anyway. The thing that always strikes me about these events is how little buying and selling is actually happening, and how many other things are going on. Dealers who haven't seen one another for a while are catching up with news, gossiping about who

bought and sold what books, showing off their recent acqui-
sitions to each other, and commiserating about the general
state of the trade. Old hands are giving advice to young tyros.
Dealers and collectors greet one another like old friends –
which they often are – and introduce each other to people
they haven't met yet. Customers show one another the things
that they've found on the stands – even when they don't intend
to buy them. The business of buying and selling becomes
almost incidental to the social event – or rather, the relationships that the social event helps to sustain are essential to
the business of buying and selling, which couldn't take place
without them.

Clubs like the Ballantyne and the Roxburghe were founded
for wealthy book collectors – although some of them left
the Roxburghe auction a lot less wealthy than they had been
when they arrived. But other versions of bookish sociability
emerged among the less well-to-do. When books were out of
reach financially, people of modest means could club together
to buy one copy between them and pass it around. A few years
ago, I was invited to the annual dinner of the Bristol Friendly
Reading Society, one of the longest-lived of these clubs. It was

founded in 1799 and is still going strong. Its members pooled their books, passed them between them and met to discuss them once several members had had a chance to read the same book. Like many such clubs, this one was originally an all-male affair, and its founding members seem to have delighted in drawing up rules and procedures, electing secretaries and treasurers, and imposing fines for breaches of conduct.

Benjamin Franklin helped to set up one such group as a young man in Philadelphia in the 1730s.[11] Franklin was determined to live frugally, and found that he couldn't spare much money for books. Without a well-established publisher in Philadelphia, many of the books he wanted had to be imported from England, which made them expensive. Franklin set up a discussion group with other aspiring young men that called itself 'the Junto'. None of them had many books, so they decided to pool their books together. They put them on a shelf in the room they hired for their meetings, and each member of the club was allowed to take one book away to read at a time. In this way, each of them got access to a lot more books than he would have had as an individual. And they all got to know each other better as they shared their books.

Over time, Franklin hatched a scheme for recruiting more readers, and getting them to pay a subscription to allow more books to be purchased. This would put the club on a different kind of footing. Instead of being a group of friends who each allowed the others to read his books, it would be a group of subscribers who purchased books held in common. In line with this new plan, Franklin started to think of the book club not just as something designed to help him and his poor but ambitious friends, but also as something that might benefit the wider community. When he went public with his plans, he helped to found the Public Library of Philadelphia. For Franklin, book clubs weren't just a convenient tool for social life or self-improvement; they were a model for how private citizens could come together to serve the public good, and an example of the kind of institutions that the new United States would need.

~~~

Benjamin Franklin visited Edinburgh twice, in 1759 and 1771. He arrived a little late to meet some of the members of another reading group, the Fair Intellectual Club. This group was founded in 1717, although most of its original members were probably still living in the city by the time Franklin got there. While his own book club, the Junto, had been for men only, the Fair Intellectuals, as their name suggests, were all young women. If Franklin did meet any of them, I think they would have hit it off, because the club's members were all around his age, and like him they were committed to their own intellectual and moral improvement. But it's unlikely that anyone told Franklin about the club, because its very existence – at least at first – was a closely guarded secret.

The first rule of the Fair Intellectual Club was that you didn't talk about the Fair Intellectual Club. Members promised 'never directly nor indirectly [to] reveal or make known, without Consent of the whole club asked and given, the Names of the Members, or nature of the Club'.[12] The membership was limited to nine young women, the number of the Muses, between the ages of fifteen (when their formal education ended) and twenty. The club's rules stated that members had to leave when they got married. They drew up reading lists and gathered to read one another 'harangues' about different topics, usually based on their reading. For young women to take their education into their own hands in this way – without supervision from men – was apparently shocking enough to require some secrecy. Despite the best efforts of scholars, the identities of these bookish young women still remain a mystery.

But someone couldn't keep a secret. When one of the members let its existence slip to a gentleman friend, the club was threatened with exposure. Rather than appear in public on someone else's terms, the Fair Intellectuals resolved to stop reading books and start writing one. The result was *An Account of the Fair Intellectual Club in Edinburgh* (1720), cast into the form of a letter to the equivalent club for men, the Athenian Society. The *Account* tells a story of friendships motivated by mutual improvement and mediated by bookish tastes. It reveals a group of young women keenly aware of the 'Disadvantages that our Sex in General [. . .] labour under' through lack of 'Order and Method in our Conversation'. They were somewhat subversively determined to remedy those disadvantages through reading books and talking about them. While the Sutherlands and other Grangerisers got together to improve their books, the members of the Fair Intellectual Club got together to use books to improve themselves.

Now it seems my daughter, who's nine, is becoming something of a fair intellectual too. She and her friends have started their own book club. They call it 'Buried in Books' (the spellings of 'buried' may vary). Like their eighteenth-century precursors, they've decided that their own shelves are not sufficiently well stocked to supply their needs. And they've noticed that if they borrow one another's books, they'll have access to a steady stream of new reading. Since they have limited pocket money to buy new books, and Christmas and birthday presents can be unpredictable, they've decided to pool their resources. They don't seem to be quite as high-minded as the young women of the Fair Intellectual Club – their tastes run mostly to *Harry Potter* and *How to Train Your Dragon*, and there's no sign of them gathering to read 'harangues' to one another so far – but they prove the point that where there are books, sooner or later there will be book clubs.

This requires some paperwork. You have to fill out a hand-written form if you want to join, and you get a handmade library card to show you're a member. These are made with coloured pencils on the back of my wife's old business cards. So far there are five members. Each of them is supposed to record loans in a notebook, although record-keeping seems a bit erratic as far as I can tell. The length of loans varies according to how long you think it's going to take you to read the book, which seems like a sensible policy I wish more libraries would adopt. You can renew your book, but if you bring it back late you have to give its owner chocolate in place of a fine.

It seems like this group of nine-year-olds has grasped many of the essential features of bibliographic sociability. They understand that books bring people together, and that sharing books can deepen existing friendships. They know that reading in groups is often gendered (there are no boys in the club) and that it tends to produce rules and paperwork of its own (hence the forms and membership cards). And they've grasped that the solitary pleasures offered by books can sometimes be enhanced by sharing them.

⌇

Of course, my daughter and her friends weren't inspired by an obscure eighteenth-century book club but by the modern ones that some of their parents belong to. By one recent estimate, 50,000 people in the UK alone belong to a reading group. These clubs are usually just casual gatherings of (typically middle-class) friends getting together in one another's homes to drink wine and talk about books. Book clubs often seem like a women's thing, and the survey of UK reading groups that Jenny Hartley and Sarah Turvey did in 1999 bears this out: 69 per cent of the groups they heard from were all-female groups, only four per cent all-male.[13] Even the mixed groups often had a large majority of women. In some cases, the groups lamented the lack of male readers, but in others they reported that efforts to include men hadn't worked well. Men, it seems, don't talk about books in quite the same way. If book clubs are mostly female spaces, this is partly because they privilege a way of talking that's often imagined as women's talk: non-competitive, non-confrontational, friendly, digressive and collaborative. The conversations book clubs thrive on are process-driven rather than end-directed: the aim isn't to convince anyone to change their view, or even to reach a consensus, but simply to hear and value the range of perspectives. In this respect, at least, book clubs model kinds of discourse that are often sadly lacking in public life.

Books connect like-minded club members, giving structure and routine to relationships that can last for years. But book clubs are also often connected to wider cultural trends. Some of the groups in Hartley and Turvey's survey followed the book recommendations of newspaper, television or radio book clubs. This took the tricky business of choosing what to read next out of their hands and made sure there were no recriminations if everyone hated the book. But even those groups who chose their own books often wanted to read the 'hot' books that everyone else was reading. They selected novels that had won prizes or received a lot of media attention. They wanted books not only to connect them with other members of the group but also to create virtual relationships with other groups across the country and beyond.

An assortment of publishers, marketers, newspaper editors, and radio and television producers has tried to cash in on this phenomenon. *Oprah's Book Club* in the US reached half a million viewers every month at its peak and helped sell an estimated $175 million dollars' worth of books. In the UK, the *Richard and Judy Book Club* on television, the Radio Four *Bookclub* hosted by James Naughtie, and the *Mail on Sunday*'s *You Magazine* book club all began in the 1990s, giving the books they featured a huge boost in sales. The many book clubs that meet in bookshops are local versions of the same phenomenon. But the obvious commercial advantages of these clubs can't explain the large number of informal clubs that have sprung up all over America and Britain. They follow no set syllabus and charge no membership fees. They reveal how books can bring people together.

So one of the things that books do for us is to help us move between being together and being alone. Often, when we read a great book, one of our first impulses is to tell others how great it was, to make them read it too, to enlarge the set of people we know who share this particular knowledge, this particular experience. We want to stop being alone with the book and start being together with others who have encountered it. And yet that sharing is a strange sort of communion. Book clubs bring people together to share an experience that each of them had alone.

The relationships that books sponsor start early and last long. And they don't stop with death. Books connect us to the dead. People now dead wrote many of the poems, plays and novels that I read, but of course I usually experience their works in new editions. But some of the books I own once belonged to dead people, too. Books themselves are durable enough to outlive the generation that produced them, becoming time capsules containing souvenirs of past readings. Second-hand or antiquarian books often come with the names of previous owners written inside. Sometimes they have formal stamps or bookplates declaring the identity of their proprietors, or marginalia showing how they used the book. These traces can open a lane to the land of the dead.

I have a book in front of me now – a volume published in London in 1898, which I bought from a second-hand bookseller in Somerset. It's not a particularly valuable or special book, but it does bear some traces of its past life, and of the lives of its past owners. Inside the front cover (on what bibliographers call the 'front paste-down') are two labels. One says 'Wiston Old Rectory' and the other 'Ex Libris Robert Booth'. The second label looks newer than the first, which is discoloured with age. But it's difficult to say with any certainty who stuck these labels into the book, or when. I don't know anything about Robert Booth. Did he live at Wiston

Old Rectory? (But then, why have two labels?) Or did he buy the book second-hand after the Rectory's inhabitant sold it?

I can imagine the hands this book has passed through in the 120 years of its existence. Perhaps it was first purchased by whoever lived in the Old Rectory at Wiston and added to his library. (Whoever this was, surely it wasn't the rector, otherwise it wouldn't be the 'Old' Rectory.) Perhaps the Old Rectory library was broken up and sold after its owner's death, at which point the book was bought by Robert Booth. Perhaps Booth's library, in turn, was sold at *his* death, and the dealer who sold this book to me bought some of the books. More likely, there were other links in the chain, people who owned the book along the way but left no label or inscription in it to record the fact. I don't know anything about them, but because they left their mark in this book, the nameless owner of the Old Rectory and the unknown Robert Booth now haunt my shelves.

They are not alone. Other ghosts linger around the bookcase. I didn't inherit any books from parents or grandparents – mine had no libraries to pass on. But I know some people whose shelves are stocked with books that once belonged to much loved family members. Often they don't read these books much – perhaps they don't share their mother's taste for romance novels or their father's interest in local history – but they don't find it easy to part with them either. They provide a link to those we have lost.

To some extent, of course, this is true of any inherited possession. A piece of jewellery or furniture would have the same effect. But inherited books offer something more – a trace of someone who was curious about, interested in or engaged by this particular book, who read it and absorbed its ideas, who valued it enough to keep it to the end of their life. These books bring into sharp focus the consciousness of the previous owner, and the fact that their consciousness has now been lost. We will never be able to ask them what they thought about this book, to tell them that if they liked this book they'll probably love this other book that we're reading at the moment. Dead people's books offer a tangible link to a time when their owners were alive and reading, as well as a reminder that this time has passed.

When you're alone with a book, you're never really alone. Not just because the characters come alive in your imagination or the author's voice rings out in your head. The book is a reminder of your relationships with other people – the people who told you about it, or those who gave it to you, or those who've already read it. And it produces new relationships – with the people you'll discuss it with, or pass it on to in turn. The people we meet through the pages of books might be people we know intimately, or those we know almost nothing about except that they owned or read this book. But every book is a potential meeting place, an agora, or even a mausoleum.

INTERLUDE

VAN GOGH:
STILL LIFE WITH BIBLE

Mourning the death of his father, Vincent van Gogh wanted to paint a picture that would reflect his sense of loss, without minimising the difficulties of their relationship. He reached for his paintbrushes, but he also reached for the family bookshelves. The result is a still life from 1885

in which two very different books stand in for two very different people. Van Gogh's father was a Protestant minister, and his Bible dominates the picture. The massive open book carries with it a ponderous authority. It is painted in muddy greys, browns and dirty whites. The text is an illegible block of smudgy brushstrokes. The volume looms against a pure black background, looking weighty, cumbersome and inert.

We can't read the open book, which perhaps suggests that it has little to tell us that is of any use, or that it offers little consolation in the face of the painter's grief. But, unusually, Van Gogh has included a legible title at the top of the page, indicating that the Bible is open to Isaiah, chapter 53. This chapter concerns the sufferings of God's servants, in a passage often understood to foreshadow the passion of Christ. Van Gogh obliquely applies this description to his father. 'He was despised, and we esteemed him not' (verse 3). It's not clear if we should understand this as a posthumous hatchet job – Van Gogh's last word on his father, spoken in words appropriated from his father's Bible – or as an act of filial remorse from a son who realises too late that he never appreciated his father properly.

In the bottom right corner of the picture, towards the front of the composition, sits another book. This one is clearly Vincent's. It is a cheap novel in yellow wrappers, dog-eared and well-thumbed. Its owner has not had it bound, perhaps because he can't afford to, or because he cannot spare the book for long enough, or because he cares nothing for keeping up appearances. The title is visible on the front of the wrapper, identifying the book as Émile Zola's contemporary realist novel *La Joie de vivre* (1884). The book connotes everything that separates Vincent from his father. It is modern, published just the previous year. It is secular, gritty and sexually explicit. It's French, reflecting Vincent's experience living in Paris and his fascination with that city as a centre of artistic culture. It's cheap, and therefore affordable to the wayward son who has yet to sell any paintings (and never would). It's thoroughly disreputable, betraying a curiosity about the seamy side of life. 'Zola in *La joie de vivre*,' Vincent wrote in a letter to his sister Willemien, 'paint[s] life as we feel it ourselves and thus satisf[ies] that need which we have, that people tell us the truth.'[1]

The way the book is painted reflects the distance between father and son. Where the Bible is a sludgy mix of browns and greys that threatens to merge into the black background, the novel stands out with bold brushstrokes of lemon yellow – a colour that Van Gogh used very sparingly at this period, when his palette was dominated by earthy tones and he had not yet begun to experiment with the brighter hues of his later paintings. The pop of colour in the foreground lights up the painting. The other possible source of light in the composition – the candlestick next to the Bible – has been extinguished in a traditional symbol of mortality. But the novel seems to be its own source of light. Metaphorically, it offers an enlightenment that the Bible cannot provide.

Van Gogh's painting uses books as badges of identity. To invest emotionally in a particular kind of book – to buy it, read it repeatedly, carry it around with you – is to signal your identity as a particular kind of person. For Van Gogh senior, the Bible is the sign of his vocation as a priest, his faith as a Christian, his cultural identity as a Protestant. It provides a guide to living, a gateway to spiritual experience, a way of structuring one's time through a programme of readings, and more. It is not just a private book but one for public use as well. It is a badge of virtue. For his errant son, the yellow novel is a sign of a very different identity: a modern, bohemian, cosmopolitan outlook that places its faith in art and literature, not in religion, and defines itself against the bourgeois piety of his father's generation. Put alongside one another in this painting, the two books symbolise the differences between their owners. At the same time, the ponderous solidity of the Bible towers over the scrappy dog-eared novel, suggesting that Van Gogh has not yet emerged from his father's shadow.

5

BOOK/LIFE

How books get woven into our lives,
from childhood to old age (and beyond)

For some of us, at least, our relationship with books starts early, usually in the lap of a parent. The warmth, the physical closeness, the drowsy pleasure of being read to at bedtime: these are early memories for many people. At first the book has few words, of course, and we read the whole thing in one go. And then we read it again. Many children ask for the same book night after night, developing an intimacy not only with the words of the story but also with the object of the book itself. Along with favourite toys, books are attachment objects. Those teethmarks on the corners are signs of affection. As the stories lengthen, lasting several nights and then several weeks, books become familiars, constant companions. I still remember my daughter's wonderment the first time we read her a book with chapters, and she realised that the story couldn't be finished in one night, but that we'd need the same book again tomorrow.

Children's books are often flamboyantly physical. Those aimed at the youngest audience – we can't yet call them readers – come equipped with touchable patches of fabric, different textures of paper, and sound-making gizmos. These are all designed to catch the attention of very young children, who usually respond with great enthusiasm: touching the textures, scrunching the fabric swatches, chewing on the pages. There's a long history of children's books experimenting with the form of the book: eighteenth-century children's books already made abundant use of fold-outs, volvelles (rotating circles of paper), pop-ups and moving parts. Some also came with free gifts or tie-in products, like John Newbery's 1770 publication *A Pretty Little Pocket Book*, which came with 'A Ball and Pincushion; The Use of which will infallibly make *Tommy* a good Boy, and *Polly* a good Girl'. As often with children's books, it's hard to tell whether this marketing puff was directed at the children or their parents, but either way it reminds us that children's books have always been keen to make the most of their materiality.

Think about one story that uses the material object of the book in a simple but brilliantly effective way: *The Very Hungry Caterpillar*, by Eric Carle.[1] The plucky little caterpillar munches his way through pages of fruit and vegetables, leaving holes in his wake. Actual holes in the pages show you where he has been. *The Very Hungry Caterpillar* has appeared in many editions since it was first published in 1969: in different sizes, on different kinds of cardboard or paper and in different bindings. But every copy of the book has to have certain physical elements, such as trimmed and drilled pages, for it to represent Carle's vision adequately. *The Very Hungry Caterpillar* is not just a story, made of words. Nor is it simply a series of pictures. And it's not just an illustrated story either. It combines words, images and book design into a composite artwork. It's a story that cannot function without its book.

Thanks, in part, to the physical properties of children's books, we are fascinated with them as objects long before we become enamoured with them as containers of information, or entertainment media, or tools we can use to get ahead. It's not just the bells and whistles that catch children's attention: there seems to be something about the printed codex itself that attracts them. In 1902, Edith Nesbit dedicated her classic children's book *Five Children and It* to the youngest of the five children in her family, John.[2] She didn't mind that he wasn't old enough to read it yet. 'My Lamb, you are so very small, / You have not learned to read at all,' she began. This wasn't a problem – she knew that the time would come when he could learn to appreciate the story. But she also knew that children love books even before they can read them. If he couldn't read the story she'd written, he would still love to handle the book it appeared in. 'Yet never a printed book withstands / The urgence of your dimpled hands,' she continued. His enthusiasm for books was a pressing desire to possess them as objects, and – to Edith's regret – it often ended up destroying the thing he desired. 'So, though this book is for yourself, / Let mother keep it on the shelf / Till you can read,' her dedication concluded.[3]

Even if you've never had a book dedicated to you, like little John, you've probably been given books, or given them to other people. You have to be careful when giving books, though. If you choose a title that leaves the recipient cold, you risk revealing how little you understand their tastes. And in China, some older people think books are unlucky gifts, because the word for 'book' sounds the same as the word for 'lose'. But for most people, books make good presents. We often give and receive books on significant occasions, using them to mark noteworthy life events. Coming-of-age occasions such as eighteenth birthdays (or twenty-first birthdays in earlier periods); religious milestones such as confirmation, first communion, or bar/bat mitzvah; educational stages such as going to high school or university – these may all be marked by giving and receiving books. In some cases, books are a central part of these events, as in the bar/bat mitzvah, when the young man or woman must read aloud from the Torah scroll, or the transition to a new school, which often involves buying new textbooks. Marriages are less commonly marked in this way, but they may be – when my wife and I got married, the minister presented us with the book from which he read the order of service. The bereaved are sometimes given books of condolence containing memories of their loved ones. At many momentous moments in our lives, books are not far away.

The anthropologist Lewis Hyde would describe these books as 'threshold gifts'.[4] These are gifts that mark the passage from one place or state of being to another. Often given as part of a ritual presentation, they are at once a way of ensuring the safe passage across the threshold, a marker certifying that the threshold has been passed, and a reminder of the experience. At the thresholds between childhood and adolescence, between singleness and marriage, between apprenticeship and qualification, and between life and death, books stand guard. The ancient Egyptians buried their pharaohs with *The Book of the Dead*, a kind of instruction manual for the afterlife designed to ensure safe passage across the frontier between life and death. In the seventeenth century and earlier it was common to read books such as Jeremy Taylor's *The Rules and Exercises of Holy Dying* (1651) to prepare for one's own death.

Books mark out the milestones of people's lives. Throughout the West, at least until the nineteenth century, people recorded the births, marriages and deaths of family members in the family Bible, a book that was often passed down from one generation to another. The practice of inscribing names and dates on the endpapers of the Bible makes the book into a worldly version of the one supposedly kept by the recording angel in heaven. When family members opened their Bible to read the Book of Malachi, they would have learned about the 'book of remembrance' that was written before God to record details of 'those who feared the Lord and who thought upon His name' (3:16). Similarly, in Revelation, the 'book of life' records the names of the saved. Writing the names of newborn additions to the family into the Bible offered a way to affirm the faith that their tiny, fragile lives were held in God's benevolence. And recording dates of death underscored the consoling belief that the deaths of beloved family members, too, were part of God's providential plan. From womb to tomb and beyond, these inscriptions say, our lives are in God's hands. Writing details of those lives into a holy book makes that faith manifest.

~~

Once we get to school, books become essential to our learning. But schools have often invested money in books, and then invested them with prestige, in a way that far exceeds their pedagogical use. Throughout the nineteenth century and into the twentieth, schools in Britain and America – as well as many Sunday schools – gave books as prizes for conduct and academic performance. In a well-known episode from *The Adventures of Tom Sawyer* (1876), Mark Twain tells the story of how Tom finagles his way to getting a coveted Sunday-school prize: a Bible earned by memorising verses of scripture.[5] Tom, who is already a notorious scapegrace, hasn't actually memorised the verses. He has traded trinkets for the tickets awarded to other children for their feats of memorisation, and so accumulated enough tickets to exchange for the prize. For, although Tom has no aptitude for applying himself to rote learning, he longs for the glory of being presented with the book. It ends badly, of course, when Tom reveals his lack of knowledge in front of the class and the visiting dignitaries there to present the Bible. But the scene reminds us that books are objects that can be endowed with prestige and that, in turn, can bestow prestige on their possessors.

That power was mobilised on a grand scale in schools and Sunday schools well into the twentieth century. Publishers produced books specially marketed to schools for use as prizes. They often included presentation pages in the front, with spaces to write the recipient's name and the occasion on which they had been awarded. These books prompted their purchasers and recipients to act in certain ways. They were valued not only for the educational or entertainment value of their contents but also as signs of achievement. At the centre of a ritual conferring prestige on selected individuals, the books were markers of distinction.

Once a year at my school, pupils, teachers and parents used to gather in the school hall for Speech Day. As I remember it, this was an occasion on which speeches were more or less incidental but books were essential. A few weeks before the event, pupils who had excelled at different subjects were given book tokens and told to buy a book and hand it in to the school office. There, the secretaries pasted in a bookplate saying to whom it was being awarded and why. On Speech Day itself, the books stood piled high on tables at the back of the stage, and pupils came up one by one to be given their book by whichever minor local dignitary had been invited to distribute them. Similar scenes, no doubt, played out in many other schools and had done for many years. The whole occasion was a ritual of amassing, marking and ceremonially redistributing books. The minor local dignitary gave a speech afterwards, but as schoolchildren we thought that the bit with the books was the main event.

Eager students spent their book tokens on improving works of literature calculated to impress the teachers. Others who were surprised to have won a prize in the first place plumped for the *Beano Annual* or something similar. And there were always a few pupils who failed to spend their book token in time. To keep the proceedings running smoothly, the school secretaries would simply grab a book at random from the school library for the minor local dignitary to hand out to these dilatory individuals on the day. This led to some awkward moments. My friend, shaking the hand of the minor local dignitary and reaching for her prize, received a book about steam trains that she'd never seen before. 'Ah, you like steam trains,' said the minor local dignitary. 'I'm very interested in steam trains myself.' 'Are you really?' said my friend, making her exit on the other side of the stage before he could engage her in conversation about the finer points of his hobby.

My friend had a lucky escape, but the fact that she apparently had to be given a book – any book – shows how centrally books as objects featured on this occasion, and how marginal their content was to the proceedings.

Books don't only feature at significant moments in our lives. They can also predict how these moments will turn out. There's a long tradition of asking books to answer questions, make prophecies or tell your fortune. The technical term for this is bibliomancy. Want to know whom you'll marry, or whether you'll get that job, or whether now is the right time to sell your house? Just open the book at random somewhere in the middle and, without looking, put your finger on the open page. There's your answer. This is possible only with a codex – it doesn't work with a tablet or scroll, or with an e-book or an audiobook. It makes use of the way the codex allows for random access (dipping in anywhere) as well as linear reading (working your way through from beginning to end). Of course, the passage you select at random is likely to need some interpretation, so half the fun is trying to apply it to your own situation in a way that gives you the answer you were hoping for all along.

You can't use just any book for this kind of do-it-yourself fortune-telling. I don't recommend you try using this one, for example. It has to be a work of wisdom or power, and preferably one already concerned with prophecy. And so there's a curious slippage here, in which the insight and inspiration of the work contained in the book get transferred onto the book itself. Muslims may use the Quran for this purpose. In China, the *I Ching* is based on an ancient divination text that can be used to make predictions or guide judgements. In the West, Virgil's epic Latin poem *The Aeneid* was a popular choice for this kind of fortune-telling, which was often called the *sortes Virgilianae* (or 'casting lots from Virgil'). Hadrian apparently tried his luck: he picked a passage that (as he interpreted it) foretold that he would be emperor of Rome. Modern appeals to Virgil's fortune-telling powers tend to be more of an ironic game than a serious ritual. But they can still be unsettling if they don't turn out as hoped. In 1639, King Charles I tried the *sortes Virgilianae* at a library in Oxford. He picked a passage in which Dido curses Aeneas, saying that he will be 'torn from his subjects' and will 'fall untimely by some hostile hand'. When the king was deposed and executed ten years later, the book seemed to have predicted his downfall with uncanny accuracy.

Over time, there was some attempt to Christianise the *sortes* by substituting the Bible for *The Aeneid*. The *sortes Virgilianae* became the *sortes Sanctorum*. In Thomas Hardy's novel *Far from the Madding Crowd* (1874), the heroine Bathsheba Everdene and her maidservant Liddy play a version of the *sortes Sanctorum* to find out whom Bathsheba will marry. Hardy presents this as a folk belief, which the unsophisticated, uneducated Liddy suggests as a bit of fun because she's bored. But it's no accident that Hardy doesn't reveal the answer the women find. The question of who Bathsheba will marry is one of the main elements driving the plot. So, in a way, when you're reading *Far from the Madding Crowd* you're engaging in a kind of bibliomancy too. Bathsheba's family Bible won't tell you who she will marry, Hardy seems to say, but, if you keep reading it, my novel will.

⟋⟍

For people who make their living from writing books, the connection between books and living runs especially deep. 'Of all the ways of acquiring books,' Walter Benjamin ironically observed, 'writing them oneself is regarded as the most praise-worthy method.'[6] For the writer, there's a special pleasure in the moment when a work finally becomes a book. After so long in the writer's mind, in his or her notebooks, or on a computer hard drive, after so many rewrites and second thoughts, so much effort and uncertainty, the work takes on material form. It turns into a thing. It's really there. I can remember quite vividly the thrill of seeing each of my books in print for the first time when they arrived from the publisher, the excitement of unwrapping the little stack of identical copies. In a way, the appearance of that thing – the published book – turns its writer into a different kind of person. Not that there aren't wonderful writers whose work remains unpublished, or who choose not to publish in their lifetimes (think of Emily Dickinson or Dorothy Wordsworth). But, in most cases, the appearance of a published book is a mark of validation that has a defining effect. Authors make books, but books also make authors.

That effect is extended when the author publishes another book, and then another. Talking to fellow novelist Ian McEwan, Zadie Smith asked 'what it feels like to look at your own bookshelves and see this nice little backlog of work. This little stack. I don't know what that would feel like. Amazing, I would think.' Recalling T. S. Eliot's character J. Alfred Prufrock, McEwan replied, 'These books are the spoonfuls with which I've measured my existence.'[7]

And yet the books on the shelf are also reminders of the distance that can open up between the book and its author. The appearance of a book in print is a sign that it has passed beyond the author's control. The time for second thoughts, redrafts and revisions is over. Now the author can only wait to see what others think of his or her efforts. As a result, authors can feel alienated from their own books, as though they are not quite the same person as the individual named on the cover. When an author's name becomes a brand name promising a certain kind and quality of product, this sense of alienation is intensified. J. K. Rowling had to abscond from her own highly successful brand by submitting a new novel under the pseudonym Robert Galbraith (although her subterfuge was soon revealed). The author's persona in the market for books diverges from his or her lived experience. When the connection between books and life seems to be most secure, it also starts to come apart.

At the end of our lives, books can be some of the most enduring legacies we leave behind us. Those of us who write books may like to imagine that we're leaving behind something that will preserve our names, our words and our ideas for future generations. Our books, we like to imagine in our more optimistic moments, will be a monument more durable than bronze – and more lustrous. Even if our dreams of greatness don't come true, though, and our books don't become classics, we can be reasonably sure that they will be stored away in the great copyright deposit libraries for the long term. In a century's time, some particularly diligent (or bored) researcher may call this book up from the catalogue of the British Library or the Library of Congress out of idle curiosity. And then, just for a few minutes or hours, my words will sound again in the mind of someone as yet unborn. Maybe. I suppose it's more likely that the book will lie forgotten on the shelves in some massive library storage warehouse, or perhaps it will survive only in a digital form. But, even so, to publish a book is to imagine not only its circulation across space but also its endurance through time. Every act of writing and publishing is thus an attempt to ward off death, to save something of ourselves from oblivion.

John Milton asserted in his 1644 treatise *Areopagitica*: 'Books are not absolutely dead things, but doe contain a potencie of life in them to be as active as that soule was whose progeny they are.'[8] The death of a book's author, he suggests, is offset in some way by the liveliness of the book. Writing books, like having children (the more common kind of 'progeny'), is a way to leave some part of yourself in the world after you die. The 'potencie of life' that books enclose has the potential to burst forth again into the life of a later reader. Milton goes on to compare books to the dragon's teeth in the legends of Cadmus and Jason, which, when planted in the ground, grow into living warriors. Books don't just get woven into our lives. In Milton's metaphor they have a life of their own, which enlivens their readers in turn.

～～

Do the dead read in the hereafter? Purified of their earthly infirmities, do they find time to catch up on the reading they never got around to in this life? Ludwig van Beethoven went deaf in middle age; his last words were supposedly, 'I shall hear in heaven.' We might imagine John Milton, who went blind, saying something similar: 'I shall read in heaven.' Or is there, perhaps, some obscure circle of hell where certain abominable writers are damned to spend eternity rereading their own interminable works as punishment for the sufferings they inflicted on their readers when alive? Fanciful speculations, perhaps. But, here on earth, books have often accompanied people after their deaths.

Sometime after St Cuthbert died in 687, his followers decided that he needed a book. They commissioned a Gospel of St John, small enough for the dead saint to hold in his hand. It was written on vellum in Latin by monks at

Monkwearmouth–Jarrow, a pair of twinned abbeys in the north-east of England, and covered in a beautifully decorated goatskin binding. The scriptorium of Monkwearmouth–Jarrow was among the most accomplished in England; just a few years later they would produce a huge manuscript of the whole Bible – known as the Codex Amiatinus – which is now the oldest surviving complete manuscript of the Vulgate. The monks of Monkwearmouth–Jarrow presented their Gospel of St John to the monastery at Lindisfarne, where Cuthbert had been the abbot. There, the monks opened Cuthbert's tomb, which had stood behind the altar since 698, and placed the book into his coffin. In the centuries after his death, Cuthbert's corpse got no peace. With his resting place menaced by Viking raids, his followers took his coffin on a protracted journey in search of safety, eventually coming to rest in Durham Cathedral. There the coffin was opened again in 1104 and the book removed. Now in the British Library, it is thought to be the oldest European book to survive in its original binding.[9] Its remarkably good condition is partly due to its long sojourn among the dead.

St Cuthbert's Gospel is – to say the least – an unusual kind of book. In the medieval period, when all books were written out by hand, it was not that odd for a book to be produced for a particular reader. Books of hours, for example, were often commissioned for elite individuals. But St Cuthbert's Gospel was produced for a reader who was already dead when production began. While Cuthbert's book didn't join him in his coffin until some years after his death, the habit of putting a Bible or other book into the coffin with the deceased was much more widespread and endured for a long time. The relationships between people and books did not necessarily end with the death of the reader. The dead often went to their final rest clutching some reading matter.

When the dead didn't literally take their books to their graves, they usually left them behind for the living. Some of my own most treasured books were given to me by old friends who have died. When I was a masters student, my supervisor was a great and eccentric scholar. He was extraordinarily knowledgeable about the subject I was writing on, and wonderfully generous with his knowledge. When my dissertation was finished, he gave me a book and wrote some kind words inside. Over the years that followed, I saw him every so often, usually in the British Library, where he would be working away on a long-planned edition. The edition was a landmark achievement. He died soon after it appeared in print. I have his edition on my shelf, and I use it frequently for my research. But I also refer quite often to the book he gave me, and every time I pull it off my shelf, I turn to his words in the front and remember him.

What will become of my books? Not the ones I write, but the ones I own. No doubt I have too many, and there will have to be some winnowing over the years ahead as I inevitably acquire more. But I'm equally certain that I'll never get rid of all my books, and that when I die I'll still own some of them. The paperbacks will probably be falling apart by then, but some of the hardbacks will easily survive me by many years. Books endure. And so – whether sold, gifted, donated or bequeathed – my books will find their ways to other owners and readers. Some of those readers will have known me well, and some will not have known me at all. If it's true that books get woven into the texture of our lives, from early to late, it's also the case that they are one of the legacies we leave behind.

John Keats had no confidence that his poetry would endure after his death. He instructed that his gravestone should read, 'Here lies one whose name was writ in water.' But, writing an informal will which he sent with a letter to his friend and publisher John Taylor, he left clear instructions for what to do after his death with the books that he had treasured during his life. The document is now in the Morgan Library in

New York. Across the top of the page, in a surprisingly strong hand for such a sick man, Keats penned, 'My chest of books divide among my friends.' It was the last iambic pentameter he ever wrote.

6

BOOK/WORLD

*How books shape institutions,
societies and nations*

I've always found something rather soothing about bookshops and libraries. The larger the better, as far as I'm
concerned. Sometimes I go to them with no intention
of buying or borrowing books and just browse the shelves.
Apparently, I'm not alone in this. University libraries report
that more and more students are coming to the library, even
though they are borrowing fewer and fewer books. Students
want to work alongside those endless shelves, even if they can
access the texts they need on their laptops. Walking down the
aisles, scanning the shelfmarks on the spines, they navigate

through corridors built of books, like bricks in a wall. But books, unlike bricks, are not exactly identical. It's the variety of books, as well as their similarity, that produces the effect. I experience libraries and bookshops as spaces of enormous potential, which invite me to imagine new avenues of intellectual exploration, new pathways of reading pleasure. But, looking at books gathered together in really large numbers, it's also easy to start feeling a kind of vertigo. In libraries and large bookshops, there's no avoiding the fact that my own reading is – and always will be – vanishingly insignificant next to the papery accumulation of books in bulk.

Libraries change the way we read. When I encounter a book in a library I experience it differently from the same book assigned on a syllabus or received as a Christmas gift. The presence of all those other books bears in on me, fostering an awareness that this book – the one open in front of me – has been selected from among many possibilities. Even a fairly modest library contains more books than most individuals can read in a lifetime. Sitting in a library with so many unread books around me, it's easy to wonder why I'm devoting my attention to this one and not to one of the others. Have I really found the book I want or need? Shouldn't I put this one down and just glance at a few others on the shelf to make sure I've chosen well? The library breaks in on the reader's absorption in the book, offering a physical reminder that to read one book is to ignore all the others that might claim our attention. At the same time, libraries make it easy to compare books, to research a topic by opening several books side by side and cross-referencing them. So, the library seems to encourage some kinds of reading, while making others more difficult to sustain.

As you browse the shelves, developing a crick in your neck from tilting your head sideways to read the titles on the spines (leaning to the right to read books published in Britain, but to the left for books from France), it's easy to feel overwhelmed by the vast amount you haven't read, and never will. Libraries and large bookshops can be paralysing, as well as empowering. One reason I leave the bookshop without buying anything is that I've been rendered torpid by the amount of choice on offer. Having picked up six or eight books that I might quite like to buy and then put them back on the shelves because I haven't really got enough money or time for them at the moment, I end up leaving empty-handed. Besides, isn't there already a large pile on the bedside table at home? Face-to-face with the bookish sublime, with books in unfathomable numbers, I find myself stunned. But no matter how extensive, no library or bookshop can hold everything. They all need some policy — whether or not it's explicitly formulated — about what doesn't belong. Like social clubs, book collections are defined as much by who or what they leave out as by what they include. And so sometimes the most interesting question to ask about a library or bookshop is: what isn't here?

~~~

Any visit to a large library reminds us that even a lifetime's reading is only a drop in the ocean of books. Jorge Luis Borges – a writer of vast erudition – was haunted by this fact. He wrote of himself as one 'who had always imagined Paradise / As some kind of library' ('Yo, que me figuraba el Paraíso / Bajo la especie de una biblioteca').[1] But in his story 'The Library of Babel', he imagined a total library containing all possible books, which is far from being a paradise. It contains:

> Everything: the minutely detailed history of the future, the archangels' autobiographies, the faithful catalogues of the Library, thousands and thousands of false catalogues, the demonstration of the fallacy of those catalogues, the demonstration of the fallacy of the true catalogue, the Gnostic gospel of Basilides, the commentary on that gospel, the commentary on the commentary on that gospel, the true story of your death[.][2]

All the knowledge you could want is there. But finding a book that is true in this library, or one that is relevant, or even one that is intelligible, is an endless and largely futile task. The suicides of the library's inhabitants, who know no other world, become 'more and more frequent with the years'.[3] The story's narrator is preparing to die in the library not far from where he was born. Borges himself kept only a few hundred books in his apartment in Buenos Aires; especially after he went blind, his connection to books was not primarily an affinity for material objects but a matter of intellectual possession.[4] Books in large numbers provoke mixed feelings. They inspire a feeling of power – so much knowledge at our fingertips! – but they also produce anxieties about how little we actually know, and how much remains unread.

The Library of Congress in Washington DC contains 167 million items on approximately 838 miles of bookshelves. It adds around 12,000 items to its collections each working day.[5] Even the most dedicated reader, with nothing else to do but read, could glance over no more than a tiny fraction of a tiny fraction of 1 per cent of the collection. New digital techniques of machine-assisted reading offer us ways of mining big datasets, providing new insights into a larger number of books than any individual or team of researchers could possibly 'read' in the traditional way. But these strategies only underline the mismatch between the capabilities of a single reader and the vast numbers of books published. And they offer a way to grapple with large numbers of texts, not large numbers of books. The library reminds us that books are not just data sources but also physical things that get stored, sorted, organised and thrown away.

Books take on new meanings when considered en masse. A shelf, a bookcase or a library of books can send messages that are different from any of the messages on those books' pages. Books have a public life as well as a private one, and they feature in our lives as citizens as well as in our existence as individuals. And books don't just reflect the nature of groups and societies but also help to shape these groups. Religious groups, for example, are partly defined by their attitude to their scriptures. Certain professional groups are defined by their access to and use of dedicated libraries (think of how lawyers use legal judgements, doctors use medical journals, and academics use research libraries). Books assembled together can reflect – and even form – the character of an individual, a group or a nation.

❧

It's not just the extraordinary number of books gathered together in bookshops and libraries that draws me to them.

It's also the organisational effort the shelves represent. Here, the books have been categorised and arranged into what Walter Benjamin called 'the mild boredom of order'.[6] As all librarians know, having the right books in the first place is only half the battle – you have to make it possible for people to find the books you have. A library catalogue, or the stock database in a bookshop, can help you find what you seek. Benjamin claimed that 'if there is a counterpart to the confusion of a library, it is the order of its catalogue'.[7]

Library catalogues have their own history, with different systems emerging to address the needs of librarians and readers in different contexts. Many heritage libraries still use what's called a 'fixed location system', in which books are shelved in relation to size and date of acquisition. This basically means that the librarians start at the top left-hand corner of the first bookcase, and then put each new book they buy on the shelf next to the last one they bought, regardless of whether the subject matter of the two books has anything in common. Larger books that won't fit on the standard shelves get their own sequence. When a shelf fills up, the librarians just move on to the next one. This means that you can walk back in time while browsing the bookcases, from the most recent acquisition to the earliest, sometimes hundreds of years ago.

More recently, many public libraries have moved over to the Dewey Decimal system, first codified in 1876, in which books are shelved by subject. Research libraries and other large libraries often use the Library of Congress system, which organises books in a complex nested set of categories and sub-categories by subject, date, author and so on. Without these classification systems, no one would ever find anything. They try to bring some structure to the amorphous collection. But this effort is always provisional, unfinished and partial. This is one reason why Alberto Manguel calls the library 'an imperfect dream of order'.[8]

Some libraries require you to look up books in the catalogue and ask for them to be brought to the reading room. But the wonder of the open shelves is that they allow you to find things you didn't know you were looking for. Serendipitous discoveries are actually made possible by clever classifications, which put the books where you can stumble across them. The arrangement of a library or a bookshop is also a tacit argument about the organisation of knowledge. By putting some books together and shelving others far apart, it makes some intellectual connections easier to trace than others, some kinds of argument easier to construct. Browse a shelf in the 'English Literature' section of a library (labelled P in the Library of Congress Cataloguing system) and you can easily see Charlotte Brontë, for example, in relation to those other nineteenth-century authors who occupy the shelves around her (Browning, Byron and so on). But if you want to see her works in relation to the history of her times, you'll need to go to the history section (labelled D), which might well be on another floor, or even in another building. Library classifications provide well-worn, natural-seeming channels in which our thoughts can flow, while actually making some kinds of thought harder to think.

Organising books also usually means putting them into some kind of hierarchy. In bookshops, the system is clear: new fiction and bestsellers by the doors for casual browsers; children's books at the back where kids can pull them off the shelves without blocking a fire exit; academic textbooks upstairs or in the basement. In libraries the hierarchy can be harder to see, but when the catalogue puts books on the same shelf, it can seem that the topics of those books are also being put in their place. The Dewey Decimal system first added topics related to homosexuality to its classification in 1932, shelving those items under section 132 (mental derangements) and 159.9 (abnormal psychology).[9] Dorothy Porter, librarian of Howard University, a historically black university in Washington DC, noticed around the same time that many libraries were putting almost everything by black writers into sections 325 (colonisation) or 326 (slavery).[10] In the Library of Congress system, among the social science books (labelled H), there's a subcategory HQ for 'the family, marriage, women', while HX is for 'socialism, communism, anarchism'. Library classification systems give the impression that they reflect an accepted order of things, shelving things together that naturally belong together. But only a little reflection reveals that they are actually making implicit arguments about the world beyond the library.

Rather than reflecting the natural order of the world around us, the ways in which librarians and booksellers organise books help to produce our frames of reference for understanding the world. Shelving books might seem like the lowliest task for the most unassuming librarians, or the humblest assistants on the bookshop's staff. Librarians working in the Library of Congress system modestly put books about books and libraries in the last classification, labelled Z, like an appendix to the world's knowledge. I dare say that's where this one will end up. But shelving books is actually the mundane iteration of an ambitious project to organise our understanding of reality. It makes some ways of thinking about the world easier and others harder.

Libraries and bookshops are social spaces. Despite their popular image as hushed cathedrals of the word, presided over by stern functionaries who shush anyone talking above a whisper, they actually have a long history of sociability. In the early nineteenth century, when private 'circulating' libraries began to open up in resort towns such as Bath, they became popular places to meet people, catch up on gossip and be seen. New arrivals in town would join the circulating library and write their names in its visitors' book as a way of announcing their entrance on the local social scene.[11] Today, larger bookshops often include cafes and stay open late. They also host events – readings, book signings and book clubs – that encourage people into the store. Public libraries, meanwhile, are pressed into service as community hubs, providing a range of services such as internet access and printing. In these ways, spaces dedicated to books play a role in social life that goes well beyond lending, selling or reading books.

Gathered together in large numbers, in libraries and bookshops, books create book spaces. At school, the kids who spend their time in the library or spend their money in the bookshop are often thought of as the conformists, the swots. But – as the swots secretly know – book spaces are often also spaces of resistance to the dominant culture. Among the books, rules and norms can be questioned. City

Lights Bookstore in San Francisco, founded in 1953, has long been an important meeting place for progressives and pro-testors. London's Gay's The Word bookshop in Bloomsbury, founded in 1979, was for a long time one of the few dedicated spaces in the UK for lesbian and gay community groups to meet. Both shops have attracted their share of legal troubles, being raided by local police in 1957 and 1984 respectively. On both occasions, police seized supposedly obscene mater-ial, and high-profile court cases followed. In these examples, places dedicated to books have brought together people and ideas in ways that have disturbed the wider culture and helped to transform it.

But book spaces don't have to be spaces of intellectual or political engagement. I once attended a wedding at the Royal College of Surgeons in London. After the ceremony, we had drinks in the library. It's magnificent, with row upon row of leather-bound books arranged along the walls and on a gallery that runs all round the room. As a specialist in the history of the book, I was quite keen to take some of them down from the shelves and learn more about them. After all, they had served generations of surgeons for their research and training. But on this occasion that was beside the point: the books lent a fine antique ambiance to the room, and that was all the guests required of them.

꙳

A library is an argument. An argument about who's in and who's out, about what kinds of things belong together, about what's more important and what's less so. The books that we choose to keep, the ones that we display most prominently, and the ones that we shelve together make an implicit claim about what we value and how we perceive the world. At McGill University in Montreal you can see a historic library that makes this point very clearly. The Osler Library of the History of Medicine was bequeathed to the university by Sir William Osler in 1919. Often hailed as one of the founders of modern medical education, Osler pioneered teaching not only in the lecture theatre but also at the bedsides of patients. Alongside his day job as a physician and educator, he was also a bibliophile who assembled a library of around 8,000 rare and historical works. He got a taste for antiquarian volumes about the history of medicine while studying and working in Europe, at a time when a number of aristocratic libraries were being sold at auction for knock-down prices. But collecting books wasn't just Osler's hobby, like fly fishing or doing crosswords. It was actually a key part of how he pursued his mission to establish academic medical education on a more rigorous footing. Over time, Osler's library grew into a resource for understanding the history of medicine. It did more than simply gather together key books on the subject; it actually helped to create the history of medicine as a subject of study in its own right.

Osler underlined the intellectual project of his library in its catalogue, the *Bibliotheca Osleriana*. There, he identified the central works in the library – the *Bibliotheca Prima* – including early printed editions of classical works attributed to Hippocrates (460–375 BCE), Aristotle (384–322 BCE) and Galen (130–c.200 CE). He shelved these works in the most prominent location in the library and surrounded them with 'secondary' books, including literary works related to medicine. During his life, Osler often entertained colleagues and friends in his library. It was a space for teaching and socialising, as well as for his private enjoyment. After his death, Osler moved into the library permanently: as he requested, his ashes are housed in the library he created, in an urn mounted between two cabinets of his most valuable books. Osler's library gives material form to his ambitions for medicine as a respected discipline of academic study with its own long and distinguished history. Implicitly, it argues that there is a distinctive tradition of writing about medicine, and claims some works as its masterpieces.

Osler's library is an especially clear example of something that all libraries do to some extent, whether we're talking about a huge university library, the library of a school or college, a local public library or the bookshelves of an individual. Libraries are the material record of decisions made by someone to buy certain books and not others, to keep some books and sell or give away others, to organise books into a particular order and so on. Bookshops reflect a similar set of decisions – influenced by a range of commercial factors and interests – to stock certain titles, to order more copies of one book and fewer of another, to offer discounts or multi-buy offers, to put these books on the tables at the front of the shop and those books on the shelves at the back, and to return unsold stock to the publisher or keep it on display.

And so, when gathered together in large numbers, books make a kind of argument that's different from the argument you find spelled out in their pages. This is an argument about what's worth reading, what's worth knowing, which books you might love, and which (implicitly) are beyond the pale, which are for adults and which for children, which are for a mainstream audience and which for special-interest groups. Walk into a library, and you find yourself in the middle of an argument about the shape of knowledge itself.

National libraries make a similar kind of argument about the values and heritage of a nation. The greatest library of antiquity, the Library of Alexandria, was founded by the Macedonian general Ptolemy I, a successor of Alexander the Great. It was a powerhouse of scholarship for three centuries BCE, and helped to make Alexandria, in northern Egypt, into a world centre of learning. The city was a major trading port, and every ship that arrived was required to give up any scrolls on board so that they could be copied for the library (although apparently the library sometimes retained the originals and returned the copies). The library was thus a clear expression of the Ptolemaic dynasty's determination to come out on top intellectually as well as militarily.

Walk into the British Library in London and you can see a latter-day version of a similar ambition. Here the nation's knowledge is on display. As you step into the building's blonde-stone atrium, bathed in natural light, a massive black cube rises in front of you, six storeys high. For a moment it just looks like a dark mass, but then you realise what you're looking at: six floors of books, six storeys of stories. This is the King's Library, housed on shelves of black wood behind tinted glass, which dominates the light central atrium. It's connected to the surrounding building by a series of narrow bridges, and if you're lucky you might see a librarian wheeling a trolley of books in or out. This is where the library keeps its founding collections, assembled by King George III (and his librarians) and by the scholars and bibliophiles Sir Robert Cotton, Sir Hans Sloane and Robert Harley. The building's design makes some of the library's greatest treasures highly conspicuous, giving material form to the knowledge of the nation on a massive scale.

What's important here is not any particular book, or even a set of books on any particular subject. Once you get close enough to read the spines, the King's Library is actually quite miscellaneous. Rather, it's the fact that so many books are displayed together – over 65,000 from George III alone – that produces the impressive effect. Their dark red, leather-clad spines (many of them bound according to the king's instructions in a workshop in the basement of Buckingham Palace) accumulate in dizzying numbers, occupying 2,438 linear metres of shelving. All the knowledge of Great Britain is here, they seem to say: massive, distinguished and unassailable. Of course, these books are only a tiny fraction of the British Library's collection. The visible parts of the library are the tip of an iceberg, whose submerged mass is the extraordinary six-storey basement, so deep that the London Underground railway runs more or less through it. This is where the library keeps many of its 150 million or so catalogued items. Many more (about 70 per cent of the total) are kept in an offsite storage facility in Boston Spa. But even though it's only a sliver of the whole, the King's Library is designed to impress. It's a synecdoche of the collection, a part that represents the whole. The dark tower of leather-bound books that confronts the visitor makes visible the collection's size and status.

⁓

Across the Channel in Paris, you can see books doing something similar. The François Mitterrand library of the Bibliothèque nationale de France was one of several *grands projets* commissioned by Mitterrand towards the end of his presidency. It stands on the banks of the Seine and holds the library's collections of printed matter. Its four huge L-shaped towers occupy the four corners of a rectangular site, looking like four giant open books. They are connected by concourses and walkways that surround a central courtyard planted with trees. Since the building opened in 1996, its users have often complained about its architecture. The four-tower design means that the book you want to consult somehow always seems to be in the tower that's furthest away. The glass and steel construction of the towers allowed sunlight to fade the spines of the books, and so blinds had to be installed. The garden in the central courtyard is not open to readers.

Despite the library's investment in cutting-edge technologies for moving books between the stacks and the reading rooms, it seems that the architects had to balance the need for an efficient and effective library with some other demands. They weren't just trying to make the library's 14 million books into a readily usable resource for the people who wanted to read them; they were also trying to turn them into a monument to French learning and culture that would be readily understandable for people who saw the library from afar but never entered it. Even those who never attempt to read the books have no trouble reading the library's message. Like the Arc de Triomphe or the Eiffel Tower, the Bibliothèque nationale is an emblem of French self-confidence. But, while the first was built of stone and the second of steel, the third was built of books.

In both these examples, the book as an object has been conscripted into national service. Arranged in unbroken ranks and often clad in uniform bindings, the books materialise the knowledge of the nation. These are copyright deposit libraries, entitled by law to a copy of every book published in Britain and France respectively, which means that the national collections have accumulated something like the totality of their nations' achievements in all fields of literary and intellectual endeavour. But their ambition doesn't stop at the nation's borders. They also accumulate enormous collections from overseas, bringing the world's books to the service of the nation's citizens. As long-established institutions, they conserve a pageant of past achievements, while as active acquirers of new material they safeguard the latest developments for the benefit of future readers. And they do all this conspicuously. In edifices built on a grand scale but structured around the object of the book, they declare volubly that the nation's achievements are bound up with its bookishness. Books, they say, equip a nation for greatness.

This is also why those determined to destroy a nation or a people often try to destroy its books. The German Jewish writer Heinrich Heine wrote in 1823 that 'where they burn books, they will end up burning people' ('Dort, wo man Bücher verbrennt, verbrennt man am Ende auch Menschen'). His words have often been remembered in relation to the Nazi book-burnings that took place in Germany just over a century later. Books are invoked in several Holocaust memorials, such as the 'Nameless Library' sculpted by Rachel Whiteread for the Judenplatz in Vienna (2000), and the subterranean installation of empty shelves by Micha Ullman in the Bebelplatz in Berlin (1995), where one of the book-burnings took place. Heine's words are now engraved on the Bebelplatz memorial. This kind of book destruction – or biblioclasm, to give it its technical name – is sadly common through much of human history. According to one story told by Plutarch (but it may not be true), the Library of Alexandria was destroyed in a fire started by Julius Caesar's army, which was besieged in the city in 48 BCE. Libraries are often casualties of war.

On 25 August 1992, residents of Sarajevo were being bombarded by the heavy guns of Serb nationalist forces under the command of General Ratko Mladić.[12] At around half past ten at night, they noticed that something had changed. Rather than blanketing the city with shells from across the Miljacka river, the Serb gunners had started to concentrate their fire on one building: the Bosnian National and University Library, housed in the city's old Town Hall. Incendiary shells pierced the roof of the building, setting fire to the bookshelves inside. The library held about 1.5 million books, including around 150,000 rare books, and 700 manuscripts and early printed books, many of them irreplaceable. As with the national libraries in London and Paris, this library was a place of great symbolic weight. Its importance went beyond the value of the items it contained, because the collection as a whole had its own significance. The residents of Sarajevo rushed to the library as it burned to save the people trapped inside, and as many of the books as they could. They were shot at by Serb forces in the surrounding hills, while flecks of ash from the burning pages settled around them like snowflakes. The rescue efforts for both books and people would continue for several days.

Neither those who set the library ablaze nor those who attempted to bring the fire under control had any doubt what was at stake. The library represented Bosnian history and culture, its collections assembled over generations. But it also symbolised the history of Sarajevo as a cosmopolitan city, home to people of different ethnicities and faiths. The library collected books in several languages, produced by both Orthodox Serbs and Muslim Bosnians, who had once worked alongside each other at the desks in its reading room. Destroying it was a way not only to eradicate Bosnian culture but also to eliminate any memory of a city in which different ethnic groups had once lived peacefully. It was an attack not only on the Sarajevo of the present, but also on the city's past. The destruction of the Bosnian National and University Library was part of a deliberate programme of attacks on cultural institutions, in which Serb nationalists targeted many other libraries. To destroy a people, it seems, you must first destroy its books. Bibliocide and genocide go hand in hand.

The ISIS forces that occupied parts of Iraq in 2014–15 understood this well. Their brief occupation was a hopeless failure in military terms, but it was a terrifyingly successful campaign of biblioclasm. Iraq has a long history of bookish culture. The country's second largest city, Mosul, is home to a university, which had a distinguished library. It had been built from donations of a number of long-established private libraries, and it was a storehouse of rare manuscripts and early printed books. In December 2014, retreating ISIS forces set fire to the library, destroying most of the collections, and booby-trapped the university campus with improvised explosive devices. The campus as a whole was ransacked, but the library was the main site of destruction. The books were targeted deliberately, as part of a strategy that ISIS has employed elsewhere of systematically destroying cultural heritage associated with other religions and other interpretations of Islam. Since the library's destruction, many individuals and institutions have pledged cash and donated books to help rebuild it. But even if the books could be replaced – which many of them can't – the meaning of the library and its destruction would not change. ISIS aimed not only to occupy Iraq's land, but also to destroy all traces of its more tolerant past.

In Mosul, as in Sarajevo, and in many other examples from conflict zones around the world, books are potent symbols of threatened identities. Assembled into libraries, they don't just give material form to the learning and culture of a particular ethnic group; they also offer a concrete reminder of how ethnic groups learn from one another and coexist through mutual understanding. Libraries' willingness to buy, store and circulate books in many languages, and from many cultures, reflects a cosmopolitan openness to other people and their ideas. The battle against books is a battle against history, against learning, against culture, against openness to others. The fact that our books stand in so readily for our identities, our aspirations and our heritage makes them targets. It's not that destroying books is a poor proxy for destroying people – an act of spite perpetrated in retreat, a scorched-earth policy for when the battle is already lost. Destroying books is a deliberate strategy for attacking the identity of a culture and denying its right to exist.

⁓

Celebrating books, by contrast, can be a way of fortifying and defending a cultural identity. In 2011, the city of Edinburgh was gripped by a bookish mystery. It began at the Scottish Poetry Library where, that March, an anonymous artist left a book sculpture on a table. It had been constructed by cutting up old books and gluing the pieces together to create a three-dimensional representation of a tree growing out of the cover of a book. No one knew who had made it. A note accompanied the book-tree identifying it as a gift 'in support of libraries, books, words, ideas'. From there the mystery spread across the city. The National Library of Scotland was the next to receive a gift – a beautifully detailed sculpture made from a copy of Ian Rankin's novel *Exit Music*. The accompanying note brought a political dimension to the project. It reiterated that this was a gift in support of 'libraries, books, words, ideas' and added '& against their exit'.[13]

Over the next few months, the anonymous artist left her works in eight more literary and cultural institutions across Edinburgh, from the Scottish Storytelling Centre to the National Museum. One seems to have been hidden so well in the Writers' Museum that it lay there for weeks undiscovered. For a while the hunt was on to identify the mysterious sculptor who gave her works away. But most people accepted that her anonymity should be respected. She later communicated by email with the Scottish Poetry Library and the Scottish Book Trust, revealing her gender but not her name. And the story had a postscript. In November 2011, eight months after the first sculpture was discovered, a final sculpture – numbered 11 out of 10 – was delivered to the Edinburgh Bookshop. Like some of the others, this one had been made from a book by Ian Rankin, and it was gifted to him personally.

The book sculptures were a celebration of Edinburgh's identity as a bookish city. Home of David Hume and Adam Smith in the eighteenth century, of Arthur Conan Doyle and Robert Louis Stevenson in the nineteenth, of Muriel Spark and Hugh MacDiarmid in the twentieth, and of J. K. Rowling and Alexander McCall Smith in the twenty-first, Scotland's capital has a long and proud literary heritage. Its central railway station is named after a novel – Walter Scott's *Waverley* (1814). It also has a rich tradition of book publishing, bookselling and book collecting. It was named the first UNESCO City of Literature in 2004. Edinburgh is a city built on books. The book sculptures set out to celebrate all this. But they also mounted a protest against cuts to the cultural infrastructure of libraries, galleries and museums, and insisted on the importance of free access to such institutions. The anonymous artist took books for both her subject and her materials. In her works, books magically transform into wondrous creations. They celebrate the ways in which books stimulate our imaginations and absorb our attention, while they also insist that books are central to a city's civic life.

INTERLUDE

BELCAMP (ATTRIB.):
GREAT PICTURE

In 1646, Lady Anne Clifford, then aged fifty-six, achieved the aim she'd been working towards since she was fifteen. She finally received the inheritance of title and property to which she had always believed she was entitled. When her father, George Clifford, 3rd Earl of Cumberland, had died in 1605, he had left his title and estates not to Lady Anne, his only surviving child, but to his brother Francis. Lady Anne and her mother petitioned the king for ownership of the estates, which they claimed were rightfully theirs, and pursued their claim through the courts in litigation of immense and protracted complexity. Only when her uncle Francis and his son had both died, leaving no male heir, did the estates pass to Lady Anne. In the intervening decades, she married twice, outliving both husbands. Her marriages had made her Countess of Pembroke, Dorset and Montgomery. But now, in addition to these titles, she was Baroness Clifford, Westmorland and Vecsey in her own right. She commissioned a painting to mark her triumph.

Books feature prominently in the painting: the so-called *Great Picture*, a triptych usually attributed to the Dutch artist Jan van Belcamp (1610–1653), which hung in Appleby Castle for 300 years, and is now in Abbot Hall in the Lake District. In the left panel, Lady Anne appears at the age of fifteen, when she was disinherited. Richly dressed, she stands in front of portraits of her governess and her tutor (the poet Samuel Daniel), next to a lute and underneath shelves of books. More books are visible, stacked on the floor. The books on the shelves are neatly arranged, some lying flat and some standing upright. Their titles are visible, and they include works by Ovid, Chaucer and Cervantes. The prominence of books in this panel is significant. It shows that alongside the customary feminine accomplishments such as playing music, Lady Anne has received a rigorous and wide-ranging education in literature, including works in several languages. Moreover, her reading has not been limited to conduct books and devotional works – the expected reading for young ladies – but has included not only foreign languages and classics in translation, but also decidedly 'masculine' authors. If her books were unexpurgated, the fifteen-year-old Lady Anne would have found in Ovid, Chaucer and Cervantes some distinctly bawdy passages.

The central panel depicts Lady Anne's parents, with her older brothers (who both died while they were still children). Books appear here too, but in decidedly smaller numbers – just three volumes stacked neatly on a shelf: the Bible, Seneca and a book about alchemy. These are safer choices. (Alchemy was one of her mother's interests, and was actually quite a mainstream topic in seventeenth-century England.) The paucity of books in this panel suggests that books were less important to her parents than they were to Lady Anne herself, and that she was the more adventurous reader. Her parents may have superintended her education but, intellectually, Lady Anne was a self-made woman. Or rather, a book-made woman. The picture suggests that by the time of her father's death she had been cultivated through her studies into a person fully worthy and capable of inheriting his title and estates, despite her gender. When the middle-aged Lady Anne gave her parents centre stage in this painting, she expressed her pride in being recognised as their rightful heir at last. But she also indicated that her merit was not only a matter of inheritance but also a result of self-cultivation through books.

Books are even more prominent in the right-hand panel, which depicts Lady Anne in late middle age, about the time the picture was painted. Now more soberly dressed (as befits a widow), the dowager countess stands with her hand on two books (one of which is a Bible) in front of more shelves full of books. Where the books in the left-hand panel were neatly shelved and stacked, those in the right-hand panel lie higgledy-piggledy on the shelves; these are clearly well-read books that get a lot of use. We know that Lady Anne continued to read regularly into her eighties, and to have books read aloud to her.[1] Her tastes had developed since her teens. The books visible in the right-hand panel include a number of works by her contemporaries; the poets John Donne, George Herbert and Ben Jonson are all there, as well as works of devotion and moral philosophy. Lady Anne had come into possession of her estates, but she had also reaped the rewards of a lifetime of reading, and she appears in this panel as a woman of erudition and good taste, as well as aristocratic status.

This triptych depicts a life bolstered by books from adolescence to late middle age. The maiden and the matron mirror one another artfully, each standing beneath her own shelves of significant books. The picture suggests how books can accompany an individual throughout the course of their life, some remaining like early and constant friends as the vicissitudes of life break over us, others discovered in the fullness of time and taken belatedly to heart. It's also significant that, while this picture was painted to mark Lady Anne's accession to her ancestral estates and titles, books take up more space on the canvas than heraldic emblems. Lady Anne was proud of her status, but here she chose to have herself depicted not only as the holder of a sheaf of aristocratic titles but also as the owner of a shelf of books. Her nobility, the picture suggests, was not just a matter of social status but also a matter of internal self-cultivation. Books accompanied her throughout her life, and made her who she was.

7

BOOK/TECHNOLOGY

*How books respond to
changes in technology*

I n November 2007, Jeff Bezos, CEO of Amazon, took to the stage at the swanky W Hotel on Union Square in New York City. He was there to talk about his plan to transform how people read. Books, he said, were 'the last bastion of analogue'. They had 'stubbornly resisted digitisation'. Amazon planned to change that with its Kindle e-reader. Three years in the making and lighter than the average paperback, it relied on new 'e-ink' technology to deliver easy-to-read text and a long battery life. The Kindle promised to do away with the eye strain of reading on backlit computer screens and offer an experience much closer to that of the paper book. But the Kindle wasn't just a substitute for the paper book; it was also a bookselling platform. It connected wirelessly to Amazon's 'WhisperNet' technology to allow users to download books from the Amazon store directly to their device. And it was a publishing platform too. At the same time that it launched the Kindle, Amazon rolled out its Kindle Direct Publishing programme, which allows authors to self-publish their work straight to the Kindle format. The Kindle took aim at the existing state of books, bookselling and publishing all at once. There had been e-readers before, notably the Sony Reader, but with this three-pronged approach, Amazon took the first major step towards Book 2.0.

While Bezos talked the assembled journalists through the features of the Kindle, he also insisted that they shouldn't pay too much attention to the device itself. The Kindle would succeed, he said, to the extent that it could disappear. Readers needed to forget that they were using it. 'The key feature of a book,' Bezos explained, 'is that it disappears when you read it. All of us readers know that flow state when we read: we don't think about the glue, the paper, the stitching; all of that goes away. All that remains is the author's world, and we flow right into that.' The Kindle had been carefully designed so that you didn't notice it. Here was an interface so effective that it wouldn't even feel like an interface at all. Readers could learn to look through it, ignoring the device and becoming absorbed in the content it delivered. 'The most important thing about Kindle,' Bezos concluded, 'is that it does indeed disappear so you can enter the author's world.'[1]

While they trumpet enhanced features that no paper book can provide, such as inbuilt dictionaries and search functions, Kindles and other e-readers remain fundamentally quite bookish. They mimic the size of printed books. They eschew the scroll feature familiar from word processors and web browsers in favour of presenting text one page at a time. Since its earliest model, the Kindle has been asymmetrical, making it heavier along one side, just as an open paper book is heavier along its spine. Meanwhile Apple, eager to compete with Amazon for the e-book market, has patented 'page-turning' software, providing animated page turns in its iPad's e-reader that closely mimic the effect of turning the leaves of a paper book. When the Kindle goes to sleep, it displays (in some versions) images that appeared originally as engravings in nineteenth-century books. In some respects, then, the e-reader is a skeuomorph – an object designed to mimic elements of another object. The operating system on our computers imitates aspects of the paper-based office, with a 'desktop', 'files' and 'folders'. Digital cameras make a noise like the opening and closing of a camera shutter when they take a photo, even though there's no shutter inside. In the same way, the e-reader imitates aspects of the printed codex. Its ability to become invisible when you're reading is based on its ability to replicate the experience of reading a printed book.

E-readers try to borrow some of the status and familiarity of the printed book, trading on our acquaintance with print to offer a reading experience that's reassuringly recognisable. By doing this, they recapitulate the early history of print. The printed codex was itself a skeuomorph. Early printed books closely imitated the manuscript books that circulated alongside them. The first typefaces resembled contemporary handwriting, and many early printed books had coloured initials added by hand after they were printed. In order to gain the confidence of readers already familiar with manuscript books, the new medium of print had to adopt some features of the existing technology. Fast forward nearly 600 years and we can see the same thing happening with e-readers, as they borrow features from the familiar form of the printed book. The end of print – if that's what this is – recalls its beginning.

These days, we hear a lot about how digital technologies threaten the book. Electronic texts and paper books are lined up as antagonists in newspaper reports about the latest e-book sales figures. Reading on the screen is blamed for the closure of bookshops. Commentators fret about how to get children to spend more time with the printed page. Journalists write memoirs of their own childhood reading that wistfully locate all that quaint papery reading in the past, in between cranking out columns that will be almost exclusively read online. In these conditions, bookish folk can start to feel under siege from the digital. Sitting down with a paper book can begin to seem like an anachronism, like wearing a watch chain.

I think there are some valid concerns here, and I'll talk about some of them in the next chapter. But I'm not really interested in promoting a heavyweight title fight between page and screen, or in betting on the winner. The new battle of the books actually conceals a far more interesting story about the history of how books have engaged with new technologies. Digital technologies are the most recent in a long line of innovations that have both troubled and enlivened bookish culture, and their story is the latest chapter in a saga that stretches much further back.

Throughout its long history, the book has assisted at the birth of several new technologies. Print got its start in the world by appearing in a book. For the pioneers of print, it was posters, forms and single sheets that paid the bills.

They were more important to the economic survival of early printing businesses than books. Johannes Gutenberg probably paused midway through printing his first Bibles so he could take on more of this kind of 'job printing', which eased his cash-flow problems and brought in enough money to pay his workmen to finish the Bible. We can even imagine an alternative universe in which printing never took off as a technology for books at all, but was confined to these other more ephemeral kinds of documents. This is what happened with later technologies like the mimeograph and the photocopier, which reproduced all kinds of documents but were rarely used for books. Fifteenth-century printers, however, invested time and resources in printing books because books were luxury products with a lot of cachet. They wanted to borrow the cultural currency of the manuscript book to promote the new technology of print. The book offered print a kind of prestige that it could never have achieved if the first printers had stuck to song sheets and forms.

When photography appeared in the nineteenth century, a similar story unfolded. William Henry Fox Talbot, inventor of the negative–positive process, described his innovations in a paper read to the Royal Institution in London in January 1839, and another read at the Royal Society a few weeks later. In 1842, the Royal Society gave him its Rumford Medal, recognising the importance of his discoveries. But Talbot didn't rely on scientific societies and their technical journals to spread the word about his new invention. He knew that if he wanted his method to be widely recognised and accepted by the public, he needed to put it into a book. He published his first efforts in photography in *The Pencil of Nature*, issued in six parts beginning in 1844. *The Pencil of Nature* took the shape of a book, but it also made books part of its subject: it included one photograph of a shelf of books and another of a page of type. Once again, the material object of the book helped a new technology to gain currency.

～～

The story of books includes technologies for moving goods and people, as well as those for circulating information. In the nineteenth century, railways spread across Europe, America and then the world. They often carried books with them. Railways moved books to retailers faster than the wagons and barges distributors had relied on before. They were good for the book market. But the benefits went both ways: books were good for the railways too. One question that sometimes bothered the Victorians was what passengers were supposed to *do* on trains. Would they have to talk to the strangers who might happen to share their carriage? Would they pass the time in enforced idleness? Would female travellers be exposed to unwanted attentions from men? (A popular pornographic novel published in 1894 was called *Raped on the Railway*.) It was a worry. But one answer quickly emerged: railway passengers could spend the journey with a book.

Bookstalls started to appear in train stations to supply reading matter for the journey. W. H. Smith and Sons opened its first outlet at Euston station in 1848 and had over a thousand station bookstalls by the end of the century. The poet and essayist Leigh Hunt produced a miscellany called *Readings for Railways* in 1849. The publisher Routledge issued a 'Railway Library' of cheap reprints. A genre of novels appeared in France known as '*romans de gare*' – 'railway station novels'. Soon, the train carriages were filled with people clutching books. Books provided a way to pass the time on a train journey, while reassuring travellers that their time was being put to good use. In the process, books played an important part in making rail travel seem socially acceptable, and easing the anxieties that it generated. The old technology of the book and the new technology of the railway found themselves in symbiosis.

Books also helped to familiarise people with how the railways worked. From 1839 onwards, George Bradshaw published his *Railway Guide*, listing timetables for trains across Great Britain. He added a descriptive *Handbook* in 1861, which included details of towns and cities throughout the country to help people plan excursions by rail. Bradshaw's volumes quickly became a feature in British households. There was even a parlour game in which people competed to plot the fastest route between two places by riffling through Bradshaw's *Guide*. Sherlock Holmes kept a copy of the book on his shelves: he asks his sidekick John Watson to consult it in 'The Adventure of the Copper Beeches' (1892). In *The Valley of Fear* (1915), Holmes and Watson have to crack a code that relies on both encoder and decoder having the same book. They quickly realise that it must be a volume 'anyone may be supposed to possess', and Watson immediately suggests 'Bradshaw'. (Holmes demurs, saying that Bradshaw's vocabulary is too limited.) So, books and railways went together like horse and carriage. The new technology of rail travel became more familiar and acceptable through its connections with the old technology of print.

<hr />

When telephones started to appear in houses and public places in the twentieth century, printed books once again helped to usher a new technology onto the stage. The rise of the phone was inseparable from the rise of the phone book. Every house that had a phone, and some that didn't, had a telephone directory listing the names, addresses and telephone numbers of everyone in the local area. Before long, separate business directories started to appear. Early on, you could call the operator and ask to be connected to someone, but once direct dialling came in you needed to know the number before you started. There's not much point having a phone if you don't know who to call, so the phone book was essential to popularising the technology.

You've seen the scene play out in a hundred movies. The private investigator in his shabby trench coat is sitting in a diner drinking coffee. The blonde bombshell who's been giving him some juicy information has just left. Stubbing out his cigarette and putting his hat on at just the right nonchalant angle, he gets up and goes over to the phone booth in the corner of the diner. There he finds the phone books, encased in their leatherette covers and attached to the shelf, as though they were in an updated version of a chained library. He opens one and flicks through it, running his finger down the page looking for the name of the schmuck the blonde's just given up. He finds the name, but he doesn't pick up the phone. Instead, he tears the page out of the book, folds it up and puts it in his pocket. He's got a lead. It's time to pay someone a visit. The scene in the phone booth became a commonplace in these movies because the phone book was such a commonplace item.

I remember it arriving every year at our house when I was growing up. I would always turn to our entry with a vague feeling of exposure and an obscure sense of pride at finding our name in a printed book. It always surprised me to see other Moles there whom we didn't know, and I would wonder if we were distantly related to them in some way. And it seemed amazing to think that you could look up all sorts of people in the book – friends, teachers, that girl from the year above at school – and find out how to call or where to visit them. The telephone was the technology that made it possible to communicate with all these people, but the book was the technology that helped you imagine doing so. And since, in order to catch on, new technologies need to seize our imaginations as well as offering us practical advantages, the phone book was essential to the phone's success.

But if the book has developed symbiotic relationships with some technologies, including photographs, railways and telephones, its relations to others have been more ambivalent. Sometimes, the closer the relationship, the greater its potential to become strained. Consider the connections between books and the technologies of sound recording. Very soon after Thomas Edison invented the phonograph in 1877, people were thinking about how it could be used to record books. That same year, the *New York Times* imagined the new technology competing with the printed book. 'There is good reason to believe,' the paper said, 'that if the phonograph proves to be what its inventor claims that it is, both book-making and reading will fall into disuse.'[2] Reports of the death of books and reading turned out to be premature, and not for the last time: in 1877 Edison's new device couldn't record anything longer than a nursery rhyme or a short poem. But the *Times*'s reaction shows us that concerns about new technologies doing away with the book are nothing new.

Blind people were the first to embrace talking books. Most blind people – especially those who had lost their sight in later life – couldn't read Braille, and so they had to rely on getting other people to read to them if they wanted to enjoy books. Until 1934, that is, when the Library of Congress set up the world's first talking-book library. It produced unabridged books on gramophone records and sent them to blind people through the mail. The following year in the UK, the

National Institute for the Blind (later the Royal National Institute for the Blind) followed suit, setting up the Talking Book Service. These initiatives were spurred on by a sense of national responsibility to those servicemen who had lost their sight in the First World War (even though they made up only a fraction of the total number of blind people). The talking-book libraries prompted debates on both sides of the Atlantic about which books should be recorded, and who should choose. Should the talking-book libraries invest their limited resources in recording improving works of lasting value, or concentrate on the bestsellers their listeners' sighted friends were talking about?

So long as people understood recorded books as primarily a charitable service for those who couldn't read printed books, there was little sense of tension. The audiences for recordings and for print didn't overlap, and so the technologies weren't competing for people's attention. But as cassette tapes and then CDs increasingly took the place of shellac and vinyl records, talking books migrated to new formats and new audiences. Duvall Hecht founded Books on Tape with his wife Sigrid in 1975 after searching in vain for some stimulating listening during his mind-numbing two-hour Californian commute. Audiobooks were no longer just for blind people; now they were for busy people too. Books on Tape identified its customer as professionally successful, affluent, educated and hard-working, with little time for reading. Soon other companies wanted a slice of the market, and the big publishing houses started to produce their own audiobooks. While talking books for the blind had insisted on reproducing the text of the book unabridged and without adornment, so that blind readers' experience would be as close as possible to that of their sighted counterparts, the new audiobooks experimented with abridgements, dramatised readings, sound effects and music.

With the arrival of digital audio formats, the audiobook metamorphosed once again. Books that had previously required dozens of records, cassettes or CDs could now be stored in a single digital file and downloaded or streamed by anyone with an internet connection. Increasingly, audiobooks started to colonise those moments when people could squeeze in some listening time, even if they couldn't read a paper book – not just while commuting, but while vacuuming, cooking or working out. Now, most people who use audiobooks are 'platform agnostic' in the industry's curious jargon. They happily move from reading paper books to listening to audiobooks and back again. In some cases, they might even do both at once: a friend told me that, finding the narrative voice of Anna Burns's *Milkman* difficult to grasp at first, she started listening to the audiobook's Belfast-accented reading while she followed along in the printed version.

From their beginnings, audiobooks have raised questions about whether listening to books counts as 'reading' – questions that haven't gone away as more and more people have begun using them. These issues came sharply into focus for me a couple of years ago when I was marking student exam papers. A student writing on Oscar Wilde's novel *The Picture of Dorian Gray* wanted to make a point about one of the characters, an actress called Sibyl Vane. The student penned a note in the margin of the exam paper, explaining that they didn't know how to spell the character's name (Vane? Vain? Vayne?) because they'd only listened to the book and not read it on paper. My first reaction was a sense of horror that the student would write about a book they hadn't 'read', mingled with grudging admiration at the chutzpah with which they admitted this fact. But then I wondered if it mattered after all. What was important, I thought, was not how the student had read the book, but what they had to say about it. I read through the answer again and gave it a high mark.

As Matthew Rubery shows in his history of audiobooks, advocates of the talking book have always tried to have their cake and eat it.[3] On one hand, they often present audiobooks as fully equivalent to printed books. They claim audiobooks offer the same experience, the same text, just delivered to your ears rather than your eyes. On the other hand, they say, audiobooks can be even better than printed books, offering something that the paperback can't hope to match. They restore the human voice to literature, adding a dimension of intimacy that's missing on the page. When authors read their own books, their voicing of the text offers insights into its meaning, or at least a sense of how it sounded in the author's head. And professional readers are sometimes just better at reading than we are ourselves — more adept at handling unfamiliar or foreign words, more adroit at managing suspense, or more accomplished at giving characters distinctive voices. In this way, their producers claim that talking books are *both* exactly the same as printed books *and* significantly better.

⊱ ⊰

This doubled rhetoric shows how complicated the relationship between books and new technologies can be. When new technologies move into bookish space, their advocates often try to make two claims at once. On one hand, they claim the new technology will disappear (as Jeff Bezos promised the Kindle would), leaving only the familiar experience of the book: you'll hardly notice the difference. On the other hand, they draw attention to the things it will do differently: you'll be amazed at how much better it is.

And yet today, when new technologies threaten to displace the printed book from the position it has long occupied in our culture, the book leaves its mark on even our most modish innovations. As entrepreneurs invent new communications technologies, they pay homage to the book – the most durable and powerful communications technology of all. When Mark Zuckerberg needed a name for his brand new social network in 2004, he turned to a book. The name Facebook recalled the printed books of photographs and basic information about incoming students that were distributed by some universities and called facebooks from the mid 1980s. When Steve Jobs called Apple's line of laptop computers Powerbooks in 1991 (and Macbooks from 2006), he acknowledged the enduring influence of the book as an object in modern society and tried to borrow some of its entrenched authority. When Intel Corporation trademarked the name Ultrabook in 2012 for a category of slim and light laptop computers, it placed these next-generation products in a lineage that extended back beyond the notebook computers they were designed to surpass to the paper notebooks from which they ultimately descend. One of the main uses of those paper notebooks, of course, was to take notes from printed books, and that's still

one of the things my students do with their notebook computers. These new things, with their bookish names, are the
latest in a long line of technologies that have intersected with
the life of books. In the vocabulary we use to talk about them,
our newest technologies continue to evoke one of our oldest.

So, far from being threatened by new technologies, the book
has often been their midwife, helping them to enter the world
successfully. At the same time, however, new technologies
draw attention to the things that paper books can and can't
do. Paper books are themselves technologies for information
storage, circulation and retrieval. Like all technologies, they
have specific advantages and limitations, distinctive features
and bugs. Thinking about the paper book alongside other
technologies brings its qualities into sharp focus.

Books produced on paper or parchment are, for the most
part, superbly durable. Given the right training in reading old
handwriting, and knowledge of the relevant languages, we can
read books that are more than a thousand years old without
much difficulty. By comparison, we have trouble recovering digital files stored only a few decades ago in superseded
formats on obsolete hardware. The printed codex offers an

interface so familiar and intuitive that we hardly register it as an interface at all. This is partly because of our early training and long familiarity with it, which makes the protocols and processes we have learned in relation to it seem natural. The codex is also, as we've seen, a powerful mnemonic apparatus, which supports our ability to remember what we've read.

But these advantages are accompanied by some limitations. For example, you can't search a printed codex very easily. Authors and publishers have developed a variety of features to improve our ability to find passages we want, such as the table of contents, the running head and the index. But digital texts allow their users to search for specific words or strings of text much faster. They also allow this kind of search query to be performed across multiple works, making finding and comparing much quicker and easier. Printed books work very well as technologies of the written word, but they cannot accommodate other media with ease. Including large numbers of high-quality colour images is often prohibitively expensive, while including audio recordings, video, or interactive data visualisations is impossible without supplementing the printed book with a website or CD. As I look along my shelves, I'm reminded of what my books can't do, as well as what they can. It's no surprise, therefore, that in our current moment of technological change the book is once again feeling under pressure from new innovations.

8

BOOK/FUTURE

What changes when books change?

Jeff Bezos was keen to reassure readers that nothing important would change when they put down their paperbacks and picked up their Kindles. But things are not so simple. Pick up an e-reader and you experience a drastically changed relationship between the material form of the book and the verbal content that it delivers. Every printed book carries only one text – the text printed on its pages. It might contain several works by different authors, as in an anthology or what bibliographers call a Sammelband – a book in which a number of separately published works have been bound together. But once a page has been printed it will never say anything else (unlike pages of vellum written on by hand, which could be scraped clean and reused). A printed codex therefore embodies a one-to-one relationship between form and content. An e-reader, on the other hand, can hold thousands of books at once, while the number of books it can potentially deliver runs into the millions. Like all modern consumer electronics, e-readers have built-in obsolescence: they are designed to fail after a certain period of time, prompting us to buy a new, updated version. But if it weren't for this fact, most people could in theory fit a lifetime's reading on a single e-reader. Where a printed codex has a one-to-one relationship between the object and the content, an e-reader has a one-to-many relationship.

This means that the material form of the book can no longer be tailored to reflect the content. Paper books take on a variety of forms, from large, heavy art books to paperback novels we can carry in our pockets. By contrast, everything looks the same on an e-reader. It doesn't matter whether you're reading Marcel Proust or Dan Brown; you're still holding the same grey plastic rectangle. But, because e-readers allow you to change the font and the size of the text, your version of *Swann's Way* or *The Da Vinci Code* may look different from mine. And e-books can readily jump from one device to another, so that we can pick up on our phones where we left off reading on our iPads. In the paper codex, the marriage of form and content was not always a happy one. But in the world of e-readers there is neither marrying nor giving in marriage. Your e-reader is a serial monogamist, dumping one text in favour of another as soon as you get bored. Your e-book is playing the field, taking up with one device after another. Form and content are no longer harnessed together in the book.

We might think that this means the book has gone from being something physical to being something virtual. An object made of paper, cardboard and glue has been replaced by a file made of computer code. But while the e-book itself may be, at bottom, all zeros and ones, the experience of reading it is still physical. E-readers are made of glass, plastic, electronic circuitry and lithium ion batteries. The electronics, which are usually made in Asia, can require toxic chemicals for their manufacture and produce hazardous waste. While it's difficult to obtain information about the supply chain for particular devices, some consumer electronics contain minerals such as coltan, which may be mined in conflict zones. The plastics used in the devices do not biodegrade, and they can enter the oceans or the food chain if not disposed of with proper care. The data that makes up the e-books themselves, meanwhile, is stored in massive data centres requiring very large amounts of electricity, some of which is obtained by burning fossil fuels. Far from being immaterial things existing in the clouds, e-books and e-readers leave their own footprint on the earth.

～～

More and more people are now reading not on dedicated e-readers but on tablets, laptops and phones. After all, who needs one more electronic device to carry around when many of us are already carrying two or even three? 'The future of digital reading is on the phone', according to former Simon & Schuster publisher Judith Curr.[1] Surveys conducted by Nielsen BookData show that the number of people who read on their smartphones more than doubled from 2014 to 2017, to 54 per cent of e-book buyers, with 14 per cent doing *most* of their reading on their phones. In both the UK and the US around two-thirds of adults and 90 per cent of sixteen-to-twenty-four-year-olds now own a smartphone. China and India are rapidly catching up, so this trend will probably continue to gather pace. This makes perfect sense – once you can access books electronically, why wouldn't you access them on the device that you carry with you all the time? But the implications are actually rather momentous. For the first time in history, large numbers of people are reading long-form texts on devices – laptops, tablets and smartphones – that were not designed primarily for reading. The relationship between the book as a parcel of content and the book as a material thing is profoundly changed.

In some respects, this can be a kind of liberation. Where print required a variety of gatekeepers – agents, publishers, printers and booksellers – who intervened between authors and readers, online text has much lower barriers to entry. The gates of the internet are open to anyone with an internet connection (although we should remember that not everyone has access to the internet). As a result, massive amounts of writing that would never have appeared in print now circulate freely online. Fan fiction, to name one popular example, has found a home in aggregator sites such as fanfiction.net, wattpad. com and archiveofourown.org. Amateur erotica also thrives online, in every imaginable variety. And large communities of memoirists, novelists and short-story writers congregate on the web. On these sites, the internet comes closest to fulfilling its promise to be a Woodstock of the mind.

People who have historically found it harder to get through the gates of traditional publishing have found the doors of the internet wide open. Digital text allows marginalised voices a space of expression. And, in some cases, self-published and digitally published books are later picked up by major publishing houses and made into paper books, providing new routes from the margins to the centre. But perhaps we should give only two cheers to new publishing paradigms as a force for social inclusion. While they allow previously marginalised voices to bypass the sentries who control access to print, they don't necessarily bring those voices into the mainstream (or allow their owners to get paid for their work). Much of this writing has a vanishingly small audience. Indeed, the very concept of a 'mainstream', a cohesive cultural centre, seems to be undermined by the proliferation of unfettered digital publishing. Online, it's all tributaries and no river.

The advent of e-books scrambles the established relationships between authors, agents, publishers, printers, publicists, booksellers and readers. In some cases, the same person might fulfil several of those roles. In others, some of the people who were essential to the printed book might be dispensed with altogether. And digital media also plays havoc with traditional publishing workflows. If you're publishing a book on paper, an enormous amount of effort goes into making sure the contents are right before the printing presses go to work. This is all worthwhile, because correcting errors or making improvements after the book has gone to press is an expensive business. By contrast, an electronic text – whether it's published on a webpage or in an e-book format – can be tweaked after publication quite easily and for little or no cost. You can put out version 1.0 and wait to see what your first readers think of it before revising it for version 2.0. As a result, electronic text is for ever unfinished, always subject to change, never set in stone.

The way we buy and own e-books is also very different from the way printed books change hands. E-book formats are proprietary: an e-book customised for the Kindle (the e-reader sold by Amazon) can't be read on a Nook (the one sold by Barnes and Noble). Publishers have responded by developing multiple digital 'wrappers' for their content, to make it available on different platforms. There's no real parallel to this in the world of paper books. Some books are confined to libraries – or even to special sections of the library – and cannot easily be read elsewhere. But the way that e-books are tied to a particular proprietary format goes beyond that – it's as though the pages of a library book magically became unreadable on the way home.

Even if you choose one provider – Amazon, Barnes and Noble, Apple and so on – and stick with them, the ways you can use an e-book are severely restricted by 'digital rights management'. E-books in proprietary formats are typically coded in a way that restricts your ability to share them, to pass them on when you've finished with them or to copy all or part of them. While e-books and e-readers remove some of the inconveniences of paper books – for example by being much lighter and less bulky, and by allowing instant delivery of new books – they also make it harder to do some of the things that we commonly do with books, such as lending, borrowing, sharing, gifting and reselling.

When you purchase a printed book, you're buying an object. It's yours to do with more or less as you wish, and it remains yours until you choose to dispose of it by selling it, giving it away or throwing it in the bin. But when you buy an e-book, what you're actually buying is a licence to access the digital file. Although your e-reader stores books on the device, allowing you to access them while offline, the seller can remove those books from your library. This happened in 2009, when Amazon removed George Orwell's novels *Nineteen Eighty-Four* and *Animal Farm* from some readers' Kindles. A company that did not have the rights to them had added the titles to the Kindle store using a self-service function, and when the rights-holder notified Amazon of this fact, they removed all copies of the books and refunded the purchasers of the bootlegged titles. Given that *Nineteen Eighty-Four* depicts a dystopian society in which information is rigorously censored, this was all deeply ironic. Amazon has publicly stated that they won't delete purchases in similar cases in the future, but the incident underlined for many readers of e-books the ways in which their continued access to the books they'd bought depended on the policies and actions of the company that had sold them. By contrast, no one's local bookseller ever came to their house and asked them to give back a paper book.

There's also some evidence that owning digital books just *feels* different from owning paper books. We've seen how people take ownership of their paper books, marking them with their names, pasting in bookplates or scribbling in the margins. And we've seen how buying and reading a book can be the start of a long relationship with it, that might involve displaying it, sharing it and rereading it in whole or in part. These are ways of bearing a book in mind and taking it to heart. We don't take possession of e-books in quite the same way. When researchers from Arizona interviewed readers in focus groups about their understandings of e-book ownership, they discovered that their informants had only limited 'proprietary feelings' towards their e-books: no one mentioned a particular digital book as an important or loved possession.[2] This partly reflects a general tendency away from buying cultural products and towards subscribing to services that give us temporary access to them – many people who once had shelves of CDs or DVDs now subscribe to Spotify or Netflix instead. But it also shows how, in many ways, our experience of e-books is just somehow thinner than our experience of paper books – more weightless, not as satisfying, less substantial.

❧

I think there are several reasons for this. In the previous chapters, I talked about the wide range of things that we do with books. Many of these things can't be done in the same way with e-books. You can't display your e-book collection on a shelf. You can't sneak away from a party to browse your host's e-books (or, at least, I don't advise trying – it leads to awkward questions). You can spend some time virtually browsing an online bookseller, but it's a very different experience from hanging out in a bookshop where serendipitous discoveries lurk around every corner. Some online library catalogues allow you to browse a virtual shelf, but scanning a list of books on screen offers a different experience from looking along a shelf of volumes in the library. You can give e-books as a gift – or at least you can give the money to buy them – but you can't inscribe your gift with words of love that the recipient may encounter again when picking up that book decades later. You can give e-books as a prize, but it's hard to imagine the prize-giving ceremony or the virtual bookplate that will record who they were given to and why.

It's difficult to pass an e-book on, and new hardware and software continually make old formats obsolete. This makes it unlikely that anyone will inherit e-books from parents or relations. You can annotate e-books, and in some cases share your annotations. But because there's no market for second-hand e-books and no incentive to develop one (quite the reverse), it's unlikely that anyone will ever acquire an e-book that bears the traces of an unknown previous reader. In the future, will nations point with pride to the size and splendour of their data centres, in the same way that they once boasted about their national libraries? Will dignitaries of the future choose to have themselves painted (or photographed, or hologrammed, or whatever) holding an e-reader as a symbol of their erudition? Will parents and children huddle together over their tablets at bedtime? Will books remain such a powerful part of our lives when they no longer have the same material form?

I don't want to be too elegiac about this. Our emotional investments in books and the various things we do with them take shape in specific social and cultural contexts, and in other contexts they could develop differently. Social science studies of the reading habits of undergraduates show that, other things being equal, they prefer to read paper books. When they use e-books instead, it's because they are easier to obtain, cheaper, and because they perceive them to be more environmentally friendly.[3] But these are still students who have grown up primarily with printed books. Most of them will have learned to read using printed books, and only later been introduced to digital formats. In the future things may be different, as a new generation grows up with digital and paper books alongside one another from their earliest experiences of books. It may be that this generation will develop – or force the corporations that sell e-books to develop – ways to gift, share, inscribe, dog-ear, inherit and resell e-books, precisely because those practices are key to how we use and value books and we find that we can't do without them. Or we may find we *can* do without them, after all, and substitute other practices for them. At this point, it's probably too early to say.

But I don't think e-books are going to kill off paper books any time soon. Much has been written about whether e-books are replacing paper books, usually prompted by the latest survey of their sales figures and market share. Behind the headlines is a more interesting story about how e-books are taking off much faster in some genres than others. Readers of romances and genre fiction have tended to adopt e-books much more readily. You can see why: these kinds of readers tend to read a lot, and they don't usually want to go back to books they've read. Many of them were probably passing their paper books on to the charity shop soon after they'd read them. These kinds of readers have moved happily to e-books. For them, in a sense, the material form of the paper book had always been an encumbrance, and they were happy to see the back of it. Readers of literary fiction, on the other hand, have been much more reluctant to make the switch. They tend to reread their books – or at least to think they're worth rereading. They are more likely to display their books on a shelf. They look for a quality package to match the quality writing inside: books of this kind tend to stay in hardback longer before moving into paperback formats. These kinds of readers prefer printed books. For the foreseeable future, we're likely to see a mixed economy, in which print and electronic books coexist.

The most momentous aspect of our current moment of media change may be that our reading devices are now increasingly multifunctional. Giving us access to books is only one of the things we ask our tablets, smartphones and laptops to do. Picking up a paper book often means putting aside the demands of work and social obligations, switching off for a while from email or the phone, and turning away from the distractions of news and shopping. But when we read on a tablet, smartphone or laptop, we usually have access to all these things and more on the same device. You can toggle continuously between your book and an email from your boss, a message from your friend, a social-media notification, a news update, or a special offer from a retailer. If you have notifications turned on, your device will continually interrupt your reading with reminders of other things you could be paying attention to.

And it's not just when I'm reading on an internet-enabled device that I experience the pull of distractions. Distraction is now our default mental condition. The media environments we inhabit shape our habits of attention. It's not that our attention spans are shrinking. By some measures they are getting longer: the average length of popular movies in 2000 was over ten minutes longer than in 1985.[4] But the properties of our attention are changing. The internet is very good at serving up gobbets of text that demand only fleeting and imperfect attention. The software we use to view webpages isn't called a browser for nothing. In conditions of massive information overload, all kinds of producers of online content know that they need to catch our attention. But only briefly: so long as we click, driving up their usage statistics, that's enough. Online, we enter the realm of the skim, the skip, the glance, the link. We browse through hundreds of options on Netflix, unable to decide what to watch. We scroll through thousands of tweets without really taking any of them in. And all the time, the kind of sustained focus and mindful attention that serious reading demands seems to get harder and harder.

Not that we are the first people to experience this sense of information overload, or to develop reading strategies to deal with it. In the past, it seems, readers had less trouble switching between modes of attention. They might skim through a newspaper in the morning, and immerse themselves in a book in the evening. Or they might distinguish between light reading, requiring only partial attention, and more serious reading, demanding greater concentration. But I wonder whether readers of the future will find it so easy to calibrate their attention to their reading matter. Our reading habits are shaped by our reading objects. The individual absorbed in a printed book was to a large extent formed by the media ecology he or she inhabited, in which the printed book thrived. The habits of attention cultivated by the codex may not survive changes in our media environment.

Or, at least, they may not survive for all of us equally. In the future, disengaging from digital media may be a luxury. While the privileged will be able to turn off their email and social-media notifications, set out-of-office messages and go on digital detoxes, an underclass will be harnessed to their smartphones by the demands of the gig economy. Over time, unplugging from the matrix for long enough to read a novel will be less and less imaginable for more and more of us. Expensive private schools will maintain large libraries of paper books, while schools in poorer areas will rely on slow internet access. And a generation raised in conditions of constant distraction won't even know what's been lost. There are genuine and reasonable concerns about whether the kind of sustained attention required for long-form, absorptive, or critical reading can survive under such conditions. On one hand, in these conditions sustained reading on paper will be a privilege, and affluent parents will pay for their children to be coached in how to do it. On the other hand, picking up a paper book might start to seem like a tiny act of resistance – an effort to disconnect, however briefly, from the constant overstimulation of online life.

Perhaps this is one reason why, now that the printed book seems to be under threat, people have started to pledge allegiance to it in various ways. The slogan 'I pledge to read the printed word' appears on many websites and blogs of enthusiastic readers. The UK's nationwide campaign to celebrate bookshops has sold and given away thousands of tote bags bearing the words 'Books are my bag'. And there seems to be a burgeoning market for T-shirts, bags, badges and pencil cases bearing bookish quotes, such as 'if a book is well written, I always find it too short' (a phrase used by one of Jane Austen's characters, but often attributed to the author herself) and 'you can never get a cup of tea large enough or a book long enough to suit me' (C. S. Lewis).[5] The proximity of death often produces declarations of love.

Despite these nostalgic reactions, it doesn't make sense to line up paper books and e-books simply as natural antagonists. Journalistic predictions about the death of the book are not just sensationalist and premature; they misunderstand how media change. New media don't simply replace old media. Printed books did not replace manuscript books. In fact, the production of manuscripts probably increased after the introduction of print. And print led to new hybrids such as the printed form that you filled out by hand. Authors well into the nineteenth century chose to circulate some or all of their works in manuscript, even when they had access to print. Others kept works in manuscript for extended periods of time before printing them. The advent of photography didn't kill off painting, although it did send it in new directions, as impressionism and then expressionism explored new artistic avenues. The CD, and then the MP3, didn't spell the end of vinyl records, which are still produced in quite large numbers today. And so there are good reasons to think that e-books will not kill off printed books.

But the significance of printed books is already changing. When buying a printed book becomes a choice, rather than simply a matter of accepting the default option, it takes on new meaning. Today, if you choose to buy a vinyl record instead of downloading an MP3, you're making a kind of declaration. It might be that you're an audiophile who finds the quality of sound reproduction on digital formats inferior. It might be that you're a DJ who wants to scratch the record on a turntable. Either way, your purchase declares that the default option doesn't suit you – and in the process reveals that no one kind of media will ever suit everyone. Perhaps something similar is happening to the printed book. Printed books aren't going away, but they are starting to take on new shades of meaning, and the choice to buy print instead of digital is gaining new kinds of significance.

To choose a print format for books when a digital one is readily available is now to declare yourself to be still committed to the object of the printed codex. It is to join the fellowship of bookish folk whose early training and subsequent experiences have attuned their reading to the printed codex in ways that they cannot simply leave behind, even if they want to. To choose to buy a paper book, when there are other options on offer, is to value its thingness, to intentionally and voluntarily invest in the particular material form it takes, and consciously to prefer that form to others. Relatedly, some publishers and booksellers report increased use of high-end features of book production that had previously been on the decline, such as ribbon page-markers, deckle edges, or so-called 'French flaps' on softcover books. Last Christmas, my local bookshop had window displays reading, 'Books make the best presents', and 'Beautiful books for Christmas'. While some readers are happy for their books to migrate into digital environments, others are becoming more concerned with their existence as material things. They want their books to be beautiful as well as functional.

~~~~~

The list of things you cannot easily do with an e-book reveals the extent to which paper books – as objects – have become woven into our lives, our relationships and our societies. To the extent that the book changes, therefore, our lives, our relationships and our societies will change too. This fact explains one of the reasons that e-books haven't already captured more of the book market. If paper books were simply machines for reading, delivery systems for streams of text, then we would happily have abandoned them by now in favour of faster, cheaper and more effective versions of the same thing, just as we've ditched telegrams in favour of emails. But there's more to the book than that. It's all the other things that we do with books besides reading them, all the meanings we invest them with, and all the imaginative work we ask them to do, that make it hard to replace the printed book with another format, no matter how closely the new format replicates the reading experience of the existing one, or how much it promises to improve on it.

Recognising the various ways that printed books have become part of our world reveals how much is at stake in transforming the book. The book has penetrated deep into our conception of the universe, at least in the Judeo-Christian tradition. Let me finish this chapter with two brief examples. Imagining God bringing judgement against the world, the author of the Old Testament book of Isaiah pictured the Creator closing up a book. Naturally, the prophet thought about the form of the book he was most familiar with: the scroll. 'All the host of heaven [i.e. the stars] shall be dissolved,' he wrote, 'and the heavens shall be rolled together as a scroll' (Isaiah 34:4). He imagines the night sky like a dark piece of parchment or papyrus, written over with stars as though with God's luminous handwriting. The heavens themselves are his star chart, which he has unrolled, and which he can roll up again when he's finished with it. It's as though we're all living in God's book.

Early in the fourteenth century, Dante reached for the same kind of image as he rose to the astonishing conclusion of his *Paradiso*, but with one crucial difference. The form of the book had changed since Isaiah's time, and Dante imagined the universe not as a scroll but as a codex. In the thirty-third and final canto, the poet finally comes face-to-face with the Deity. Gazing on the divine presence (in C. H. Sisson's translation), he 'saw gathered up in the depths of it, / Bound up by love into a single volume, / All the leaves scattered through the universe' (lines 85–7). Speaking of such things, Dante necessarily relies on the imaginative resources of poetry, on simile and metaphor. The book is the metaphor he reaches for. The book, in its various forms, hasn't just provided the delivery system for our most profound thoughts about the universe and our place in it; it has also sometimes supplied the language and imagery that shaped those thoughts and gave them voice.

Dante's image of the leaves lovingly bound up together into a book (*legato con amore in un volume*) marks the difference between how things seem to us on earth, and how they are revealed to him in Paradise. We experience the world as a jumble of 'accidents and their relations' (*accidenti e lor costume* (line 88)), without any apparent order or meaning, like so many loose pages scattered to the winds. Dante's own poem would have been copied out by scribes working in teams, so that each one saw only a portion of the poem. Before it could be understood, the different quires of paper they had worked on had to be bound together in the right order. As with the book, so with the universe: God's love brings the orphaned fragments of our experience together, orders them and binds them up into an intelligible whole. God is the binder and the binding at once. It's his love that makes the scattered scraps of broken lives cohere into a beautiful and meaningful creation.

In the final moments of the final volume of Dante's *Divine Comedy*, the poet reminds us of the book in our own hands. The beatific vision is also a bibliographic one. Our most familiar reading tool is transfigured into an image of the universe itself – and an image that was not available to the author of Isaiah in the same way. The shift from the scroll in

Isaiah's day to the codex in Dante's had provided a new way to understand the Creation. A new relationship between the linguistic content of the book and its physical form doesn't just produce a new reading experience; it signals a much more widespread realignment that has the potential to change our identities, relationships, education, institutions and societies – even our conception of the universe. Changing the book means changing the world.

Coda

BOOK/END

Soon after we moved into our flat in Edinburgh a few years ago, we found a joiner to make us a new bookcase. This was to be a momentous investment, not just because of the money it cost – which turned out to be quite a lot – but because it held out the possibility that, at long last, all of our books would be arranged in some sort of order and displayed where we could easily pluck them off the shelves at will. The books had been out of reach for a number of months, boxed up in a storage unit that I never visited. I imagined that moving them onto their new shelves would usher in an era of happiness and felicity, in which I would stop fretting over misremembered facts and half-remembered stories and simply walk over to the bookcase and extract the book I wanted, turning to the right page with scarcely a pause in thought or conversation. Once the books were on the shelves, I would surely become happier and more productive – and we would truly have arrived in our new home.

The joiner helped to foster this benign fantasy. As he wielded his tape measure, he told me proudly about the bookcases he had built for a well-known novelist, a wealthy collector, and an esteemed scholar. He asked all the right questions about the kind of books I owned – how many were there, of what size, and so on. He convinced me that, yes, the cost of bespoke bookcases was well worth it. I needed them – deserved them, even. As weeks of delays stretched into months (his supplier had let him down, his apprentice had gone off sick, he'd taken on too many orders at once, the bookcase just needed to be painted, it would definitely be done by next week) I started to have my doubts. But when the bookcases finally arrived I thought they looked very fine. I shook his hand as I passed over the cheque.

In those months of relocating across the Atlantic and coming to rest in Edinburgh, my books reasserted their existence as things. Every one of them needed to be handled and packed. Instead of lining the walls of my study, they constructed a wall of cardboard boxes that took up most of the floor. Packing up my books took a long time, not really because there were all that many books, but because there were so many pauses along the way as I reacquainted myself with books I hadn't looked at for a while. There were hard decisions to be made about which books to pack and which to sell or give away. As I started to pay attention to how many boxes my books would fill, how much they would weigh, how much space they would take up in a shipping container, and how much it would cost to move them across the ocean and store them until we had houseroom for them, their unavoidable materiality came home to me once again.

When the new bookcases arrived, my daughter – who was then four years old – took great delight in helping me open the boxes of books and pile the volumes all over the floor: novels over here, history books over there, poetry somewhere else. She learned the word 'prose' (at first, she thought it had something to do with 'crows'). Her pleasure in handling and stacking the books seemed undiminished by the fact that she couldn't read them. Soon the piles started to totter and had to be divided into subpiles. But how? By author, by subject, by date of publication? Eventually we decided on a rough plan. It had to be rough because there were so many books that didn't quite seem to fit into any of the categories we'd established for them, and so many exceptions that it seemed prudent to make. And then, once we started to put the books on the shelves, we encountered another problem (one all too familiar to professional librarians). Just when I was halfway along a shelf of twentieth-century poetry, say, I would pick up a book that was too tall to fit. Should I separate this book from the others with which it belonged, or relocate all the twentieth-century poetry books to a taller shelf just to accommodate this oversize volume? Again, the materiality of the book asserted itself.

To be honest, the pleasure of unpacking my library was also tinged with shame. I felt a little ashamed to have spent so much money on books over the years, when others have so little to get by. It seemed self-indulgent and unreasonable to want my own copies of books that were readily available in libraries. I felt guilty about hanging onto books I hadn't looked at properly for years, and might never reread in their entirety, when I could have passed them on to others. I felt sheepish about owning so many books and remembering so little of what I had read in them. Even as I luxuriated in the thought of having my own little library all set up around me, I was reminded that owning books, or even having easy access to them, is a privilege from which many are still cut off.

As the books moved slowly from the floor onto the freshly painted shelves, they reminded me how tightly they are sutured into my sense of self. Separated from them as they crossed the ocean on a cargo ship, I had felt adrift. Now we welcomed each other into a new home. The bookshelves, built to fit the wall of the living room, were a statement that we planned to stay in this flat for some time. It's unlikely that we will be able to take them with us when we move again. The books ranged along them display facets of my identity. You can see the subjects that interest me, the books that bear most signs of rereading, the authors whose complete works I wanted to have and those who are represented by only one volume or none at all. And even if you don't stop to read the titles on the spines, or to take a book down from the shelf and open it, you can still see that I am the kind of person who values books. Other people's walls are adorned with sports memorabilia, or photos of themselves with important people, or certificates of their qualifications, or shelves of vinyl records, or antique china, but I have none of these things: my walls are covered with books.

Books belonging to my wife and my daughter share the shelves with mine, and with a number of volumes that belong to all of us equally as our lives as readers and book owners become intertwined. Over the years, our books have got increasingly mixed up, so that sometimes we don't know who first bought and read a particular volume. At the same time, shelves of books belonging to one or other of us reveal areas where our enthusiasms don't overlap. Bookshelves are not only an index of an individual mind but also a record of lives lived together.

When people visit us, I notice which shelves they linger over and which they glance past. Some people, inevitably, want to know how many books there are (I'm not sure) and whether I've read all of them (more or less). Some home in on a particular volume they want to look at. Others regard the bookcase as just another piece of furniture and pay it no attention. Sooner or later, with many of our friends, the conversation turns to books, as we compare what we've been reading, recommend titles and authors to one another and, in a variety of ways, use books to communicate and relate to one another.

As I flicked through some of my books, I rediscovered notes and scribbles in the margins that I had made years before. They were like messages from a past life. They revealed the ways in which I had taken possession of these books, marking them for my own. The kinds of marks I'd made, and the extent of them, showed how I had approached different books. Some were heavily marked up, with passages underlined on almost every page, comments in the margins, summaries at the end of each chapter and notes jotted on the endpapers. Others had no markings at all – these had usually been read for pure pleasure, with no expectation beyond a few hours' amusement, and no thought of referring back to them later. The annotations were notes to my future self, scaffolding for my faulty memory, and reminders of how I had related to this particular book. And reading them again was like hearing from my past self – sometimes earnest, sometimes puzzled, sometimes naive – as I worked out my own thoughts in relation to the author's.

It took a lot of rejigging the organisation, with many pauses along the way to glance once again into this or that volume, but eventually all the books ended up on the shelves, with more on the other bookcases in the bedroom and the study. Finally, all my books were arrayed in splendid order. Contemplating the serried spines, I realised that I was also looking back over my life. Each book represented hours spent reading, while whole shelves disclosed enthusiasms for a subject or an author that had waxed and waned, as well as some that still endured. There were books that I'd bought twenty years before and moved from one flat to another ever since as their spines slowly faded in the sunlight. Some had been recommended to me by old friends I'd now lost touch with. Some had been given to me on significant occasions, others read on memorable holidays or forgettable flights. As I looked along the shelves, memories of bookshops and reading experiences came back to me. Every volume was a remembrance of things past.

But I looked to the future too. There was still some empty space on my new shelves, ready to be filled with the books I would read over the coming months. My daughter, who was just starting to learn how to read for herself, would no doubt add some books of her own to the shelves. I thought about what I wanted to read next – what gaps in my knowledge I hoped to fill, what new projects I aspired to undertake and what kinds of pleasure still awaited me among the pages of books. The unoccupied bookshelf offers a space of possibilities, an undiscovered country. As I thought about how the still-empty shelves would one day be populated, I understood that my new bookcases would be full soon enough, that some of the books on them would need to be weeded out, finding their way to new owners and other libraries. And I realised – with a little thrill of horror – that one day the collection as a whole would have to be broken up. The books that I'd been assembling, storing, organising and reading for all these years would leave the shelves when I died, or downsized, or just needed the money, and find themselves once again circulating in the world.

In doing so, those books would continue their journey through the world of things. Even a private library is not entirely private. Books have a social life of their own. Each printed volume is one of many similar ones, which may number in the hundreds or in the millions. And so each volume is connected to other volumes, circulating through other hands, and each owner or reader is connected to the owners and readers of those volumes. To own a book (especially one that you could borrow from a library) is to insist on having a private relationship with it. But to own a book is also to join a collective, to become part of the public for whom the work has been published. Some manuscript books were produced for a single owner, but printed books are always produced for a group of some kind, however large or small. As texts, my books bring news from the world: they are full of insights into the experiences of people in other times and places. But as objects, they also link me to the world: they create material connections between me and other readers. There's a special pleasure in seeing a copy of a book you own on someone else's shelf. At first the sighting brings a mild shock of recognition – isn't that my book? And then it brings a warm feeling of connection, as one reader of that work recognises another.

When my daughter grows up, I wonder if she will feel any need for built-in bookcases in her living room. Even if she shares my enthusiasm for books and reading, it may take a very different material form for her. Brought up with texts on paper and on screen before she could read them, it seems unlikely that she'll have the same dedication to the printed page, or that paper books will become as central to her identity as they are to mine. Perhaps she will glance fondly down the list of files in a virtual library stored on a server, or invest her money in a high-end e-reader. Or perhaps she'll give up on the idea of the book altogether, and do her reading not in discreet bookish units, but by dipping into a vast liquid continuum of online text.

But whatever technologies she uses for reading, her books will have a physical existence as well as a purely linguistic one. They will have material form as well as immaterial content. Whatever else it is, the book is a thing. While the particular material form that books take changes over time, the fact that they have a material form does not. Not even when part of that material form is hidden in data centres far from view. Not even when we access words through devices that we use for lots of other things besides reading. To encounter books is always to encounter a physical object that is burdened with meanings.

Once the books were all on the shelves, and the cardboard boxes that had sheltered them for the last few months were folded up and put out with the recycling, we felt that we'd finally moved into our new flat. We started to invite more people over, as we made friends in our new city – including some booksellers, academics and librarians, whose professional lives are bound up with books. A librarian friend, coming into the living room one evening, said, 'Ah! Here are the books', as though they were something he'd being looking for since he arrived, a topic of conversation he'd been waiting to get around to, the solution to a conundrum. His eyes scanned along the shelves looking for something to pique his interest. He singled out one book, reached up and pulled it off the shelf, with a librarian's careful touch. He hefted the book in his hand, feeling its weight before he opened it. The book left a gap behind on the shelf, an empty reminder of its presence, which closed up slightly as the adjacent books relaxed into the available space, as though they were breathing out.

ACKNOWLEDGEMENTS

I'm very grateful to Francis O'Gorman, Alberto Manguel, Heather Mole and Simon Spanton-Walker, who read complete drafts of the manuscript and offered valuable advice. Beverly Rogers and William Zachs generously allowed me to view their collections. Alison MacKeen read the manuscript at an early stage and offered crucial encouragement and practical wisdom, while Danielle Bukowski helped guide me through the publication process. I'm grateful to Jennie Condell, Pippa Crane and Jill Burrows, who all helped to bring the book into publishable form. Thanks are due to my hosts and audiences at the University of Otago; the University of Nevada, Las Vegas; Brigham Young University, and Lyon and Turnbull Auctioneers, Edinburgh, where I gave early versions of parts of the book as lectures. I've also benefited enormously from conversations with generations of students on the MSc in Book History and Material Culture at the Centre for the History of the Book.

NOTES

1.   *The Letters of Charles Lamb*, edited by Thomas Noon Talfourd, 2 vols (London: Edward Moxon, 1837), vol. I, p. 115.

I Book/Book

1.   The French theorist Roland Barthes called these meanings 'mythologies'; Roland Barthes, *Mythologies* [1957], translated by Annette Lavers (London: Vintage, 2000).

2.   Arjun Appadurai (ed.), *The Social Life of Things: Commodities in Cultural Perspective* (Cambridge: Cambridge University Press, 1988).

3.   Gilbert Ryle, *Collected Essays: 1929–1968* (London: Routledge, 2009), pp. xvii–xviii and 479–510.

4.   There are a number of good introductions to the history of the book. See, for example, Michelle Levy and Tom Mole, *The Broadview Introduction to Book History* (Peterborough, Ontario: Broadview, 2017); James Raven, *What is the History of the Book?* (Cambridge: Polity, 2018) (which I have drawn on for information given here about the global spread of printing); Amaranth Borsuk, *The Book* (Boston, Massachusetts: MIT Press, 2018); Keith Houston, *The Book: A Cover-to-Cover Exploration of the Most Powerful Object of Our Time* (New York: Norton, 2016); Michael F. Suarez, S. J. and H. R. Woudhuysen (eds.), *The Book: A Global History* (Oxford: Oxford University Press, 2013).

2 Book/Thing

1. Martin Heidegger, *Being and Time*, translated by J. Macquarrie and E. Robinson (Oxford: Blackwell, 1962), especially pp. 102–7.

2. Marcel Proust, *On Reading* ('Sur la Lecture', 1906), translated by Jean Auret and William Burford (New York: Macmillan, 1971), p. 5.

3. Thomas Hardy, *Far from the Madding Crowd*, edited by Suzanne B. Falck-Yi (Oxford: Oxford University Press, 2002), p. 95.

4. Anne Fadiman, *Ex Libris: Confessions of a Common Reader* (London: Allen Lane, 1998), pp. 31–6.

5. Leah Price provides a wonderful overview of the different uses for books in Victorian Britain in *How to Do Things with Books in Victorian Britain* (Princeton, New Jersey: Princeton University Press, 2012).

6. Patrick Leigh Fermor to Artemis Cooper, 23 February 1982, in *Dashing for the Post: The Letters of Patrick Leigh Fermor*, edited by Adam Sisman (London: John Murray, 2016), pp. 351–2.

7. The letter is reproduced in the foreword by Gioacchino Lanza Tomasi to Giuseppe Tomasi di Lampedusa, *The Leopard* (London: Vintage, 2007).

8. Nelson Goodman, *Languages of Art: An Approach to a Theory of Symbols* (Indianapolis, Indiana: Hackett, 1976), especially pp. 112–26.

9. Thomas De Quincey, 'Lake Reminiscences, No. IV: William Wordsworth and Robert Southey' in Julian North (ed.), *The Works of Thomas De Quincey*, vol. 11: *Articles from* Tait's Magazine *and* Blackwood's Magazine, *1838–41* (London: Pickering and Chatto, 2003), pp. 110–31 (pp. 117–18).

10. Ann Blair, *Too Much to Know: Managing Scholarly Information Before the Modern Age* (New Haven, Connecticut: Yale University Press, 2010), pp. 213–29.

11. Heather Jackson, *Marginalia: Readers Writing in Books* (New Haven, Connecticut: Yale University Press, 2002).

12. See, for example, the one discussed by Stephen Orgel, *The Reader in the Book: A Study of Spaces and Traces* (Oxford: Oxford University Press, 2015), p. 44.

13. Andrew Motion, *Philip Larkin: A Writer's Life* (London: Faber and Faber, 1993), pp. 485–6.

3 Book/Self

1. The classic history is Henry Petroski, *The Book on the Bookshelf* (London: Vintage, 2000).

2. Richard Holmes, *Shelley: The Pursuit* (London: HarperCollins, 2nd edn, 1994), p. xii.

3. Milan Kundera, *The Unbearable Lightness of Being* (London: Faber and Faber, 1985), p. 48.

4. Ibid., p. 47.

5. Johann Wolfgang von Goethe, *The Sorrows of Young Werther*, translated by David Constantine (Oxford: Oxford University Press, 2012), p. 7.

6. Robert Southey to Charles Watkin Williams Wynn, 22 June 1805, in Carol Bolton and Tim Fulford (eds), *The Collected Letters of Robert Southey*, A Romantic Circles Electronic Edition, www.rc.umd.edu/editions/southey_letters, accessed 2 February 2018.

7. Jules Verne, *Twenty Thousand Leagues Under the Sea* (New York: Scholastic, 2000), p. 77.

8. Leon Watson, 'All the Comforts of One's Home: Rare Glimpse of Queen's Life at Balmoral Explained', *Telegraph*, 21 September 2017.

9. Charlotte Mosley (ed.), *In Tearing Haste: Letters Between Deborah Devonshire and Patrick Leigh Fermor* (New York: New York Review Books, 2008), pp. 100–104.

10. Gary Urton, *Signs of the Inka Khipu: Binary Coding in the Andean Knotted-String Records* (Austin, Texas: University of Texas Press, 2003); Marcia and Robert Ascher, *Code of the Quipu: A Study in*

Media, Mathematics and Culture (Ann Arbor, Michigan: University of Michigan Press, 1981); see also Roderick Cave and Sara Ayad, *A History of the Book in 100 Books* (London: The British Library, 2014), pp. 20–21.

11. Alberto Manguel, *Curiosity* (New Haven, Connecticut: Yale University Press, 2015), pp. 74–81.

12. Jane Austen, *Northanger Abbey*, edited by Barbara M. Benedict and Deirdre Le Faye (Cambridge: Cambridge University Press, 2006), p. 259.

13. For an overview of this aspect of the science of reading, see Simon Liversedge, Iain Gilchrist and Stefan Everling (eds.), *The Oxford Handbook of Eye Movements* (Oxford: Oxford University Press, 2011).

14. Gemma Walsh, 'Screen and Paper Reading Research: A Literature Review', *Australian Academic and Research Libraries*, vol. 47, no. 3 (2016), pp. 160–73; doi.org/10.1080/00048623.2016.1227661.

4 Book/Relationship

1. Lucy Peltz, *Facing the Text: Extra-illustration, Print Culture and Society in Britain 1769–1840* (San Marino, California: Huntington Library Press, 2017).

2. Mario Curreli, 'Remembering Borys Conrad (1898–1978)', *Conradiana*, vol. 12 no. 2 (1980), pp. 83–7 (p. 86).

3. Dante, *The Divine Comedy*, translated by C. H. Sisson, *Inferno*, Canto V, lines 127–42 (Oxford: Oxford University Press, 1993), pp. 68–9.

4. John Keats to Fanny Brawne, 4 July (?) 1820, in Robert Gittings (ed.), *Letters of John Keats* (Oxford: Oxford University Press, 1970), p. 383.

5. Edward Bulwer-Lytton, *Pelham: The Adventures of a Gentleman*, edited by Jerome J. McGann (Lincoln, Nebraska: University of Nebraska Press, 1972), p. 310.

6. Leslie A. Marchand, *Byron: A Biography*, 3 vols. (London: John Murray, 1957), vol. II, p. 811.

7.   Andrew Motion, *Philip Larkin: A Writer's Life* (London: Faber and Faber, 1993), p. 319.

8.   The book is catalogued at BL Kings MS 9. For the page with Henry's inscription, see http://www.bl.uk/manuscripts/Viewer. aspx?ref=kings_ms_9_f231v.

9.   Philip Larkin, *Selected Letters of Philip Larkin: 1940–1985*, edited by Anthony Thwaite (London: Faber, 1992), pp. 46–7.

10. Walter Benjamin, 'Unpacking my Library', in *Illuminations*, translated by Harry Zohn (London: Fontana, 1992), p. 67.

11. *Benjamin Franklin's Autobiography*, edited by J. A. Leo Lemay and P. M. Zall (New York: Norton, 1986), p. 63.

12. *An Account of the Fair Intellectual-Club in Edinburgh: In a Letter to a [sic] Honourable Member of an Athenian Society There* (Edinburgh: James McEuen, 1720), p. 7. The club has been discussed by Derya Gurses Tarbuck, 'Researching an Early Eighteenth-Century Women's Intellectual Club', *The Center and Clark Newsletter*, no. 48 (Fall 2008), pp. 4–6; Derya Gurses Tarbuck, 'Exercises in Women's Intellectual Sociability in the Eighteenth Century: The Fair Intellectual Club', *History of European Ideas*, vol. 41 no. 3 (2014), pp. 375–86; and Clifford Siskin, *System: The Shaping of Modern Knowledge* (Cambridge, Massachusetts: MIT Press, 2016), pp. 206–21.

13. Jenny Hartley, *The Reading Groups Book* (Oxford: Oxford University Press, 2002), p. 25.

Interlude/Van Gogh: *Still Life with Bible*

1.   Leo Jansen, Hans Luijten and Nienke Bakker (eds), *Vincent van Gogh – The Letters: The Complete Illustrated and Annotated Edition*, 6 vols. (London: Thames and Hudson, 2009), Letter 574.

5 Book/Life

1.   Eric Carle, *The Very Hungry Caterpillar* (New York: World Publishing Company, 1969), and many, many editions since.

2. The eldest three children were born to Edith and her husband Hubert Bland; the other two were fathered by Bland with Edith's friend Alice Hoatson. All five children and three adults lived together.

3. E. Nesbit, *Five Children and It* (London: Virago, 2017).

4. Lewis Hyde, *The Gift: How the Creative Spirit Transforms the World* [1979] (Edinburgh: Canongate, 2012), pp. 44–5.

5. Mark Twain, *The Adventures of Tom Sawyer* [1876], edited by Shelley Fisher Fishkin (Oxford: Oxford University Press, 1996, 2010), pp. 42–52.

6. Walter Benjamin, 'Unpacking my Library', in *Illuminations*, translated by Harry Zohn (London: Fontana, 1992), p. 63.

7. 'Zadie Smith Talks with Ian McEwan', originally published in Vendela Vida (ed.), *The Believer Book of Writers Talking to Writers* (San Francisco: Believer Books, 2005), pp. 207–39; reprinted in Ryan Roberts (ed.), *Conversations with Ian McEwan* (Jackson, Mississippi: University of Mississippi Press, 2010), pp. 108–33 (p. 133).

8. John Milton, *Areopagitica*, in *The Complete Prose Works of John Milton, Volume II: 1643–1648*, edited by Ernest Sirluck (New Haven, Connecticut: Yale University Press, 1959), pp. 480–570 (p. 492).

9. Claire Breay and Bernard Meehan (eds.), *The St Cuthbert Gospel: Studies on the Insular Manuscript of the Gospel of John* (London: British Library, 2015).

6 Book/World

1. Jorge Luis Borges, 'Poem of the Gifts' ('Poema de los Dones'), in *Selected Poems*, edited by Alexander Coleman (London: Penguin, 2000), pp. 95–8.

2. Jorge Luis Borges, 'The Library of Babel', in *Labyrinths*, edited by Donald A. Yates and James E. Irby (London: Penguin, 2000), pp. 81–2.

3. Ibid., p. 85.

4. Alberto Manguel, who read to Borges as a young man, reports these facts in *Packing My Library: An Elegy and Ten Digressions* (New Haven, Connecticut: Yale University Press, 2018), p. 48; see also Alberto Manguel, *With Borges* (London: Telegram, 2006).

5. Figures from https://www.loc.gov/about/fascinating-facts/, accessed 15 March 2018.

6. Walter Benjamin, 'Unpacking my Library' in *Illuminations*, translated by Harry Zohn (London: Fontana, 1973, 1992), p. 61.

7. Ibid., p. 62.

8. Manguel, *Packing My Library*, p. 76.

9. Doreen Sullivan, 'A Brief History of Homophobia in Dewey Decimal Classification', *Overland*, 23 July 2015; https://overland. org.au/2015/07/a-brief-history-of-homophobia-in-dewey-decimal-classification/, accessed 20 March 2018.

10. Zita Cristina Nunes, 'Cataloging Black Knowledge: How Dorothy Porter Assembled and Organised a Premier Africana Research Collection', *Perspectives on History: The Newsmagazine of the American Historical Association*, November 2018.

11. See Lee Erickson, *The Economy of Literary Form: English Literature and the Industrialization of Publishing, 1800–1850* (Baltimore, Maryland: Johns Hopkins University Press, 1996), pp. 125–41.

12. See Matthew Battles, *Library: An Unquiet History* (New York: Norton, 2003), pp. 184–90.

13. The story is told by an anonymous author in *Gifted: The Tale of 10 Mysterious Book Sculptures* (Edinburgh: Polygon, 2012).

Interlude/Belcamp (attrib.): *The Great Picture*

1. Several scholars have examined the evidence of Lady Anne's reading. See Stephen Orgel, 'Reading with the Countess of Pembroke

and Montgomery' in *The Reader in the Book: A Study of Spaces and Traces* (Oxford: Oxford University Press, 2015), pp. 138–57 and Heidi Brayman Hackel, *Reading Material in Early Modern England: Print, Gender and Literacy* (Cambridge: Cambridge University Press, 2009).

7 Book/Technology

1. Quotes from Jeff Bezos taken from the liveblog of the event at https://www.engadget.com/2007/11/19/live-from-the-amazon-kindle-launch-event/, accessed 12 March 2018.

2. 'The Phonograph', *New York Times*, 7 November 1877, p. 4.

3. Matthew Rubery, *The Untold Story of the Talking Book* (Cambridge, Massachusetts: Harvard University Press, 2016). I've drawn on Rubery's excellent book throughout this section.

8 Book/Future

1. Quoted in Jennifer Maloney, 'The Rise of Phone Reading', *Wall Street Journal*, 14 August 2015.

2. Sabrina V. Helm, Victoria Ligon, Tony Stovall and Silvia Van Riper, 'Consumer Interpretations of Digital Ownership in the Book Market', *Electronic Markets*, vol. 28 (2018), pp. 177–89 (p. 183).

3. Naomi Baron, *Words Onscreen: The Fate of Reading in a Digital World* (Oxford: Oxford University Press, 2015), especially pp. 83–4.

4. The average length of the 25 most popular movies released in each year, according to data from the Internet Movie Database, analysed by Randal Olson and reported in Sidney Fussell, 'Are Movies Getting Longer? Here's the Data', *Business Insider UK*, 14 June 2016.

5. Jane Austen, 'Catharine, or the Bower', in *Juvenilia*, edited by Peter Sabor (Cambridge: Cambridge University Press, 2006), p. 249. The quotation from C. S. Lewis is reported by Walter Hooper in the preface to C. S. Lewis, *Of Other Worlds: Essays and Stories* (San Diego, California: Harvest, 1975), p. v.

INDEX

INDEX

ABOUT THE AUTHOR

Tom Mole is Professor of English Literature and Book History at the University of Edinburgh, where he runs the Centre for the History of the Book. He has taught at universities in the UK and Canada, and has lectured widely in Europe, Australia and North America. He has written or edited several volumes about books and literature, including *What the Victorians Made of Romanticism*, which won the 2018 Saltire Prize for Research Book of the Year. He lives in Edinburgh with his wife and young daughter.